Watching My Hands at Work

A Festschrift for ADRIAN FRAZIER

Edited by
EVA BOURKE
MEGAN BUCKLEY &
LOUIS DE PAOR

Salmon

Published in 2013 by
Salmon Poetry
Cliffs of Moher, County Clare, Ireland
Website: www.salmonpoetry.com
Email: info@salmonpoetry.com

ISBN 978-1-908836-54-0

COVER ARTWORK: *Benjamin de Burca*
COVER DESIGN, TYPESETTING & LAYOUT: *Siobhán Hutson*

PRINTED IN IRELAND BY *Sprint Print, Dublin*

**This publication was grant-aided by the
Publications Fund of National University of Ireland Galway /
*Rinneadh maoiniú ar an bhfoilseachán seo trí Chiste Foilseachán
Ollscoil na hÉireann, Gaillimh***

*Salmon Poetry and the editors would like to offer their thanks to
Thomas Dillon Redshaw for his support of this publication.*

CONTENTS

INTRODUCTION

It is now more than twelve years since Adrian Frazier arrived from the United States to teach in the English Department in NUI Galway at the height of a distinguished and varied career as a literary scholar whose fields of research and expertise lie in the area of nineteenth and twentieth century Irish prose, poetry, drama and cultural history.

Glancing at his formidably long list of publications, which includes a comprehensive biography of George Moore (*George Moore: 1852-1938*), a detailed and very entertaining study of John Ford's close collaboration with the Abbey's crew of actors and directors in Hollywood (*Hollywood Irish: John Ford and Abbey Actors in the Movies*), several book publications edited or co-edited by Adrian on various aspects relating to Irish poets and dramatists, as well as countless papers, articles and reviews on a wide range of topics to do with the work of Irish poets, playwrights and film-makers, it quickly becomes clear that Adrian is not only knowledgeable about his subjects but that his approach is also invariably original and thought-provoking.

Keeping in mind that he had been actively involved in drama productions and had published poetry in the past, it is not surprising that his attitude to education should be holistic and diverse, providing for instruction that is not only theoretical but also hands-on, practice-based and creative, and that as a consequence he set up a taught MA in Drama and Theatre Studies in 2000, followed by an MA in Writing two years later.

Convinced of the educational value of postgraduate programs in which students explore their place in the outer world as well as their emotional responses and their sensations creatively, he structured the MA programs in such a way that aspiring writers are given the opportunity to discover their individual talents and passions and to work with a great sense of fulfilment. Both MA programs are practice-oriented, the plays written throughout the year are produced, directed and acted by the students themselves, and the MA in Writing offers, uniquely among similar programs in the country, the chance of trying out a variety of genres, from poetry, to fiction, to screenwriting, to non-fiction, in order to allow the students to find out where their own particular interests and strengths lie.

These MA programs constitute a resource of universally-educated spirits capable of imaginative solutions, people who might have continued, or will continue on to other careers, academic or otherwise, who have grown in confidence, empathy and flexibility of mind, and are able to draw on their experiences of creative practice as well as on academic perspectives.

This Festschrift, *Watching My Hands at Work*, consists of poems, short stories, essays and extracts from novels and plays written by graduates of the MA in Drama and Theatre Studies and the MA in Writing, by tutors teaching in the programs over the years and by practitioners of the art from inside and outside Ireland who came to speak of their own personal experiences of writing and publishing to the participants. It has been put together to honour and celebrate the invaluable contribution Adrian Frazier has made to education and the arts in NUI Galway and further afield in the literary community of Galway and Ireland as a whole.

When thinking of him the words that come to mind immediately are integrity, tolerance, generosity and passion. The enthusiastic response to our call for submissions attests to the gratitude and love felt by so many towards Adrian—particularly current and former students. Moreover, this Festschrift is intended to highlight and celebrate the 10th and 12th anniversaries of the M.A. in Writing and M.A. in Drama programmes, respectively. Long may they continue and thrive.

THE EDITORS

Watching My Hands at Work

David Wheatley

IN GLENMALURE

Crimson our halberds from the gore of the Saxons!
The firebrand soon secured and our sword arms aching.
Affliction our foes' part and Fiach McHugh O'Byrne
honoured at the pig feast by rivers of mead;
shrill from the dark high glen the bleating of sheep
while in and out of the mist floats Lugnaquilla.

The Castle styles Michael Dwyer a common killer
and, be it hereby known, will spare no expense
in his apprehension. Caught, this felon will ship
to New South Wales there to lament, ochone,
at his leisure his exile from old Wicklow amid
Fenians who barely 'scaped hanging like Billy Byrne.

An old man I passed by the monument to the O'Byrne
deep in the glen, his face a sunburnt colour,
had about him so melancholy a mood
I felt the spirit of that mountainous expanse
convert us, strangers, into almost kin
in that quiet corner where a man could sleep.

Early one morning a fair maid I met on the slope
of Ballinacor, her dark eyes heavy with brine
from weeping for her dear one unjustly taken,
the blackbird of sweet Avondale who would call her
his *leannán*, his darling from the tree-top in accents
so soft that for that want of them she was unmade.

Farmyard cottages ready to view, all mod
cons, no chain. Give the recession the slip
where money doesn't swear, it talks sense.
Take in the pine woods' late autumnal auburn
round picture-postcard-pretty Lugnaquilla
between the waterfall and perennial bracken.

Driving down into Glenmalure, not speaking,
the road flooded, the wheels spinning in mud:
O Fiach McHugh! Waiting for the shower to clear,
getting out, walking, feeling the damp seep
through my boots down the accursed boreen
where I revved and tried in vain to turn on a sixpence.

And crueller than all weather loom again
those peaks on the line of the sky that still drive mad
the woebegone sheep astray where the gorse fires burn.

Molly McCloskey

from CIRCLES AROUND THE SUN: IN SEARCH OF A LOST BROTHER

(Penguin 2011, with kind permission)

My father walked crab-wise. From the waist up, he listed to one side as though assailed by a strong wind. He was eighty-two and had scoliosis. As he sidled across the gleaming mid-court of the Palace in Auburn Hills, Michigan, he looked like someone who had just got out of bed and was hamming up his aches and pains. His second wife and five of his six children sat in a semicircle behind him.

It was 2008. I had come to Detroit for the weekend from Paris to help celebrate the high point of my father's career. In 1979, after a few drifty years during which it looked like his NBA career might fizzle out (he was fifty-three by then, there weren't a lot more chances left), my father took one of the least coveted jobs in the league, as general manager of the Detroit Pistons. For decades the Pistons had been one of the worst teams in the NBA. The year he took over, they won sixteen of eighty-two games. Within a few years, my father had, through a series of clever and controversial trades and draft picks, turned the team into contenders and rescued himself from the brink of professional oblivion.

By the time he left the club in 1992, the Pistons had made five trips to the Eastern Conference finals and three to the NBA finals, and had won the NBA championship in 1989 and 1990. The second of those titles was won against the Trailblazers in the Coliseum in Portland. Until that series, Detroit hadn't won a single game in Portland since 1974—the year my father was fired as coach of the Trailblazers—and so to win the title there, the scene of so much frustration for my father a decade and a half earlier (the final game clinched at the buzzer, on a shot with 0.7 seconds left on the clock), must have tasted especially sweet. After the Pistons won their first championship, my father said to me, 'How many people can say they're the best in the world at something? You can't measure that if you're a surgeon. But we can say that right now we're the best in the world at what we do.' He wasn't bragging, just stating a fact. Actually, he seemed humbled by his good fortune.

During my father's tenure in Detroit, the team acquired the sobriquet Bad Boys because they played, depending on your point of view, either tough and aggressive or just plain dirty. In the book *The Franchise: Building a Winner with the World Champion Detroit Pistons, Basketball's Bad Boys*, Cameron Stauth called it Coalminer Style, in reference to my father's roots. Now, the architect of the Bad Boys was being honoured. At half-time of a Pistons game, a banner with my father's name on it would be raised to the rafters. For us—his children—there was an added resonance to the occasion. This was the first time since the divorce, thirty-one years before, that the five of us had come together to see him. For the thirteen years he had lived in Detroit, and over the few subsequent years he'd lived and worked in Minnesota, I had never once visited him in his home.

How had that happened? Was it my decision? Was I ever invited? I can't remember. By 1989, I had moved to Ireland, meaning that my father's habit of visiting us when he happened to be in town on business—scouting, usually—didn't apply. Five or six years passed during which I didn't see him at all. Aside from Mike, who my father says kept him for years on a list of people he didn't want to see, I saw less of him than any of my siblings did. I would read about him in the paper and find myself slightly surprised to be reminded that there was someone out there in the world with whom I shared so much of my DNA.

Throughout the weekend, I kept noticing my father's hands. As a child, I'd been intensely aware of them: square and thick, callused, the plentiful hairs like wire. That these hairs should sprout in the spaces between his knuckles had struck me as fabulously animalesque. I have memories that specifically concern his hands. He had a habit of drumming his fingers on the table-top in time with a tune (he'd played the piano all his life), producing a deep thrum that with my skinny girlish digits I couldn't replicate. And the way he held a tumbler of vodka and tonic and, with the index finger of the same hand, stirred the drink, imprinted itself on my mind as masculine and authoritative, signalling an easy command of the physical universe.

The hands were still square and strong, unchanged, really, from what I remembered, their familiarity deep and uncanny and also disconcerting, for they called attention to how much he was otherwise changed. Though it had only been two years since I'd last seen him (we'd played tennis; his frustration with my erratic forehand hadn't lessened), he was otherwise dramatically diminished. He spent the weekend flanked by three or four massive black men, all former players of his who looked like they might at any minute burst out of their designer suits. He appeared almost childlike among them. (One of the four was Vinnie Johnson, who had sunk the winning jump shot against Portland in 1990.) But it wasn't my father's seeming smallness, or even the recent drastic increase in the curvature of his spine, that was most striking. It was the eyes. They had long had a slightly sad cast to them, a look suggestive of unexpressed emotion; now they were rheumy and bloodshot, giving him a lost and abstracted, even frightened, look. It was the look of incipient senility, and it lent him an air of vulnerability that was totally incongruous with the person he had been. This was the guy who'd told me, 'I always say that my business is the business of winning.' This was the guy who'd said, 'A winner is a loser who just didn't quit.' Now he was a man who looked, at every moment, as though he were trying not to cry.

On the night of the banner-raising, there were speeches at halfcourt. My father's own contribution was brief. He singled out a few of his contemporaries for praise—his scouts Stan Novak and Will Robinson, the Pistons' owner Bill Davidson, and Chuck Daly, who my father had hired to coach the team. Of the four, one—Stan—was already dead. Stan and my father had known each other for over sixty years; they'd been at Ie Shima together in 1945. Of the other three, Will would die four weeks later. Bill would die in March the following year. Two months after that, Chuck would die of pancreatic cancer.

After he spoke, my father was led over to a photo collage commemorating his achievements. The collage was unveiled by two ample-breasted blonde cheerleaders wearing shiny white pants and halter necks. He was instructed to pull a curtain rope to reveal the banner, his name against a white background, trimmed in the team colours. The banner rose to the rafters as rousing triumphalist music blared. Every time I watch the YouTube clip—his crab-wise walk that looks excruciating, his doe-in-the-headlights expression, the faltering voice—it is that music that finally brings tears to my eyes.

The previous night, we had all attended an informal dinner for my father, along with Chuck and some of the players from the Bad Boys era. Everyone who wanted to say something about my father was invited to do so. Following a panicked flurry of nods and whispers, we decided that Tim would speak on our behalf. It was not an easy task, and Tim was a risky choice. He has always been the most unselfconsciously good-hearted among us. But his interior monologue tends to be exteriorized, and so he is the one most likely to blurt out precisely the wrong thing. He pulled it off, though. He told a story of when he was ten and went to basketball camp and was greeted by a now-famous coach with a growling, 'You'll never be as tough as your old man.' A generic enough tale pitched to the crowd at hand (a crowd for whom toughness was the ultimate attribute) and tinged, ostensibly, with admiration. For those of us who knew better, it was also an unwittingly sad anecdote, for it was a reminder of how deeply in my father's shadow all his sons had felt.

Towards the end of that evening, the five of us kids ended up sitting around one of the tables with my father. He signalled that we were all to join hands. Six of us in a circle holding hands, as though we were having a seance. He squeezed the hand on either side of him and his eyes filled with tears. We knew he was going to say something deeply sentimental. He is the opposite of my mother, who, though a warm and caring person, is astonishingly devoid of sentimentality, whom I have never once seen shed a tear through all of our miseries, or through her own. My father, on the other hand, can tear up at the slightest hint of emotion, particularly when he says, 'I love you.' Or, his more emphatic, signature phrase, 'God, I love you.'

The eyes of his five children darted from side to side, in our swapped glances a mix of apprehension, sentiment, slight embarrassment at this weird public display, and the temptation to giggle. But we summoned the necessary gravitas and waited for whatever was to come. Finally, my father said, 'This one's for Mike.'

If there is anything that binds us to our father, it is basketball. There is a strange photo taken in our rec room in North Carolina when I was about three. I am perched on the coffee table—an upturned tree stump my father had converted into furniture. My father, my sister Robin, John and Timmy are sitting in a row on the sofa, facing me. My father is holding a basketball, offering it to me as though it were a sacramental object. I am eyeing him with what looks like dubious reluctance, showing no sign of taking the ball. (It looks, in fact, like it would be too heavy for me to hold.) My three siblings stare expectantly at me. A huge amount appears to be riding on my acceptance or refusal of the ball.

He saw me play once in college. When he met me outside the locker room after the game, I burst into tears, ostensibly on account of my poor performance but really in the throes of a much more fundamental anxiety: the fear of love's conditionality. His old friend Stan Novak, the Pistons' scout, was with him, and I can still see the look on Stan's face: tender and wide-eyed. Stan was a softie. My father's expression, a forgiving and somewhat abashed smile, suggested that he thought my tears disproportionate to the situation. We both knew that my performance on the court was essentially irrelevant; by then it was clear that I was not going to crash through some glass ceiling and become the first woman to dunk the ball, or even develop into a college player of minor significance. I suppose I should have felt relieved, but instead I felt adrift. If we weren't linked by this, then by what?

That weekend in Detroit we had a minibus for the family and the friends of my father's who'd come for the weekend from out of town. As we drove between the hotel and our various activities, I felt sad and oddly envious. It seemed to me that my father and I were essentially where we had been when I was eleven—neither closer nor further apart—and yet so much had happened to him since. It was as though at some unconscious level I had assumed that, because he hadn't added to *our* story since 1976, he hadn't added to the story of himself. But his life had had a whole second act. By 2007, he had been married to his second wife for nearly thirty years. His best friends were people I had never met or even heard of. They spoke of him intimately, drawing on a store of recollections that none of his children could match.

I had last seen my father in 2006 when I'd visited him in Georgia to talk to him about Mike. We sat in the office in his house, surrounded by photographs, trophies and memorabilia, including an autographed photo of Babe Ruth, a home-run ball Steve had hit in a Little League game when he was twelve, and a framed crayon drawing I'd made at the age of four, depicting the heads of several ladies who had just been to the hairdresser's—a drawing my father had hung over various desks and dressers since the day of its creation. He had told me that he was glad I was writing about Mike and that he wanted to help. Like my mother, he seemed to feel that it was a form of tribute. But when the time came for us to talk, he was guarded and slightly ill at ease. It was understandable. This was the first time we'd ever set out to have a conversation about Mike.

My father had seen him about a year before, when he was out in Oregon. 'He gave me a big bear hug before I left,' he said, and I thought of the way Mike had held on to me when I left him in the lobby of Shari's the week of Tim's wedding. He said that Mike had talked about his days playing ball at McGuinness and about the Catholic League championship. In fact, much of what my father told me about Mike that day was linked, in some way, to basketball. During Mike's first year at Duke, when he was playing on the freshman team, my father only got to two of his games, because Wake Forest usually played on the same nights. My father's impression—not shared by everyone—was that although Mike had been happy to play that first year, he wasn't disappointed when it was over.

'He knew he wasn't good enough for power schools,' he said. Then he smiled sadly and shook his head. 'But he sure could shoot the ball.'

When Mike was finishing high school, my father had hoped that he would choose a smaller college where he could play regularly. He still wondered whether it might have anchored him and kept him away from the drugs he always implicated in Mike's demise.

My father didn't think that, apart from the usual arrogance of college students, Mike changed for the worse during his years at Duke. It had never entered his mind that there were mental problems. Nor did he believe that there were indications of any problems growing up. He saw a boy who studied hard, got good grades, had friends. 'Mike might've been a little serious,' he said, 'but he was a normal kid.'

I asked him about a story I knew only dimly, about his having bailed Mike out of jail in the mid seventies. Mike was drifting on the east coast then, living in boarding houses or sleeping rough. One day my father got a call from the Durham police department saying that Mike had been arrested on the Duke campus.

'What was he arrested for?' I asked, afraid to hear the answer.

'Vagrancy,' my father said. 'He was shooting baskets in the gym.'

My father flew from Oregon to North Carolina, making his way to an old dilapidated jail where he found Mike in an enclosure made of high chain-link, more like a cage than a cell. With him in the cage were about a dozen big black guys. Nearby, there was another cage full of women. Two of the women were fighting over one guy, and all the guys could see this and were picking sides and cheering. The place was chaos. Mike—skinny, scared, disoriented white boy—looked at his father and said, 'Dad, get me out of here.'

My father shook his head and chuckled at the memory, not because he took the jail scene lightly but because it wouldn't be in him to offer an explication of the pain it caused him. Instead, the sadness is embedded in the humour, implicit and bearable. The story, if told properly—with affection and elan—provides adequate cover. And my father loves a good story. When he tells one that involves himself, particularly one in which he has done something silly, he manages to render his incompetence charming, implying that proficiency in such a situation would be somehow *womanly*. And he has done some silly things. Like setting his own pants alight (it was 1973, they were polyester) while attempting to get the fire in the den going by adding lighter fluid to it. He didn't know there was a difference between a reluctant barbecue and a log fire. He is rigid in his way, and fanatically disciplined, but he can laugh at himself. And it was with a similarly bemused exasperation that he recalled some of the scrapes Mike had got himself into.

There was another incident he described which I must have witnessed myself, though I have no memory of it. It took place at a Trailblazers' game in Portland in the mid seventies. My father recalled that he was just taking his seat on the bench following a time-out when he spotted a guy coming into the arena, wearing a long green army coat with big brass buttons. He had unkempt hair and a scruffy beard. The whistle blew. My father turned his attention back to the game, not even registering who it was he had seen until he felt a tap on his shoulder and heard a familiar voice behind him saying, 'We gotta get you out of here. We have to go.'

He turned around and found himself staring into the mad eyes of his own son.

'I can't leave now,' my father said. 'Go sit with Mom in the stands.'

'No,' Mike said, 'you have to get out of here.'

My father hadn't seen Mike in some time, but he was hardly in a position to have this conversation; he had enough on his plate—in the middle of a game, in the middle of a losing season, holding on to his job by a thread.

Later that night, he took Mike for a walk on the golf course and Mike got down on his knees and wrapped his arms around my father's legs. It was the sort of thing nobody does in real life, a flamboyant enactment of filial piety straight out of Shakespeare or a film about the Cosa Nostra. He pleaded with him, 'If you don't get out of coaching, you're going to have a heart attack.'

My father blamed it on the drugs. It was a neat and simplifying explanation, one that allowed for the conclusive denunciation of all that he had found troubling about the last several years. The self-indulgent hedonism of the young. Their blithe disregard of the sacrifices of past generations. The way they ridiculed the country he loved while living off the fat of its prosperity. He looked at his son, down on his knees in the wet grass, the old army coat, the wild eyes, and saw the madness of the last decade embodied.

Sandra Bunting

TROPICAL WINDOWS ON A GREY CANAL

Lime-green windows moved
into a shocked neighbourhood
and set off sightings at suspect places
like the university and on the canal
with a fishing rod and a canoe.
There was talk. There is always talk.

What went on behind those curtainless
key lime windows? Attempts
by desperate locals to know thwarted:
the postman running from terriers,
front view obstructed by sultry palms,
the wall at the back canal too high.

A dandy was seen placing
pots of magnolias out front.
Did he have a beard? He must
have, because he wore sandals,
and was definitely the type
to put his feet up in public.

In the green of spring-time the front door
burst open to let out a parade of girls
with long skirts and tresses, imagination
wild as a north Ontario landscape,
sophisticated as a strand of cultured pearls,
himself in the background orchestrating it all.

Sandra Bunting

ACAULINE
after Irving Layton

Don't waste your life
scorning gentle souls
or fear what softer
poets say about you.

It may never
occur to them
to comment on
your privates:
they have their minds
on other things;
not all on this planet
is sex and war.

Nor do all poets spend
their time wondering
if nuns in cloister
masturbate in unison,
voices behind the altar
in ecstasy over
the body of Christ.

But if they do,
take it like a man
for the greater good,
exalt in lines penned
to leave you limp

and sweating.
Get into it and bask
in the privilege
that anyone would
think enough of you
to write a poem
with you in mind.

Ndrek Gjini

MY FATHER

My father is 88.
Yesterday I got a letter from him.
He said he is not feeling very well lately,
as in these last six months
he lost four friends
and three teeth.

Ndrek Gjini

A LETTER FROM MY FATHER

My dear son!
Thanks for the invitation,
but I can't make it.

It's spring time now,
you should know that,
I am too busy.

The snow just died
and I have to go to its funeral.
Leaf buds are going to be born soon,
and I have to attend their birthday parties.

After that,
the flowers are going to have
their wedding celebrations,
and you know that
I can't miss these beautiful events.

Last month, I got an invitation from death,
and to be honest I told it that I couldn't go.
It's spring time …
Sorry!
I am too busy right now.

Ken Bruen

A TALE OF TWO CHILDHOODS

As a child, I was guilty of the worst crime in the Irish calendar: I was quiet. In fact, I never spoke and those who know me now wonder if maybe I wasn't a better gig then.

Moving on.

Sitting beside me was a lad named Gerry, full of vim and vigour and as they say, even then *most likely to succeed*.

Right behind us was a lad named Sean, from the poorest area of the town and to be poor then meant watching for the rent man on a Friday night and alerting your mother to turn off the lights so he might believe you were out.

As if there was anyplace to go.

And *lights out* didn't convince the rent man of anything, save, you hadn't paid the light bill.

Fast forward.

Gerry, two years ago, hadn't quite become the success they'd planned and the circus was in town and, a few pints the worse, he went down at four in the morning to pet the tigers, as he felt they might be lonely.

They took both his arms off.

It was indeed, dare I say, tabloid *fodder*.

He was front page for all of a day. Got over thirty large in compensation.

With the help of new friends, he blew the money in five weeks.

I ran into him last year when my French translators were in town. (See, see the casual way I inserted that, like I have whole realms of translators and last year, it was the turn of The French.)

I was in the bathroom and Gerry came in, asked me to, em, help him to relieve himself. He had refused any artificial limbs, telling me,

"Them yokes never fecking work."

I'm thus engaged when the translator walks in and not only am I...*manhandling*...but with a person who is obviously physically handicapped.

My dark rep in France was...SOLID.

Gerry asks me to light him and I put a cigarette between his lips, fire him up and he goes,

"How are them books doing for you?"

And my heart is scalded, torn in a thousand ribbons, and I know the sheer decency he was raised in, I say,

"Doing okay now, thanks."

And armless he moves off, ensconced in a cloud of nicotine, says,

"You were always a hoor for them books."

I met Sean last week, he had just been named as the third richest man in Ireland, ahead of Bono and trust me, that is serious bucks or Euros or whatever you measure in, and he is just about the coldest person I've met in many an era and believe me, I've met some cold ones: most of them I'm related to, more's the Irishe-d pity, mainly through alcohol, and he says,

"I don't read fiction."

Right off the bat, like I'd asked him,

"Do you read fiction?"

Subtext here: *do you read me?*

None of that false bonhomie,

"Gee, haven't seen you in twenty years, how the devil are you?"

No wonder he's rich.

Reminded me of the old adage, if you want to know what God thinks of money, look who he gave it to… Madonna?

I muttered something along the lines of,

"Hasn't Ireland changed so much?"

Piss poor, you think I don't know?

And then the moment: he gives me the full-on eye fuck, says,

"But I've read your most recent offering."

Don't you love him?

I wait, cos waiting is what – not so much what I'm best at, but what I'm most accustomed to, and

he's used to making pronouncements and then, he adds,

"You need to write a bestseller."

Got it.

Memo to self.

Wake up, say yer prayers, have a shower, ring your child before she goes to school and, em, write bestseller.

I have it.

When I was young, the old people, they'd see some poor afflicted soul, they'd bless themselves, utter,

"There but for the grace of god..."

I think about that and guess what, when I utter that, who do you think I see as the afflicted soul?

Hint: when I had to go to hospital after I got me jaw broken at a book launch, who came to see me, said,

"I'd have brought a book but I couldn't carry it."

Jordan Smith

TALKING ABOUT THE TAOIST PRECEPTS WITH ADRIAN FRAZIER

… Give up learning and put an end to your troubles

We can't. But since when is good advice that goes unheard
The *Tao* that *can* be told?—not the eternal walk along
The strand, each new footfall an act of balance
In the awkward, glinting, shifting stuff of it, the lark's
Warbling, meaningless and pleasing just by that,
None of that "irritable reaching after fact," and no
Ideas in the emptiness of things passed or past.
Be like a reed, the precepts say, and you're thinking
Of the trout at the current's margin, flecked and sipping
In the weeds (*be*), while I'm hearing some finicky,
Raucous instrument suddenly finding tune, the split
And doubled tongue (*a reed*) resolving, a sad
Philomelan voice and a drone suggesting that maybe
The point is *like*, resemblance teaching what learning can't
Acquire here among the rushes in a world of splendidly
Unnerving almost-rhymes (*rush* to *lush* to *loss* to *less* to
Summer's *lease*) we only have to half-remember
Since everywhere the reminders flock, call, and gyre.
Listen, we heard them once, the snippets, these
Brief bouts of wisdom, and though the studious might
Have set about transcribing them for posterity,
We watched the tide erase the plovers' tracks
And that was enough to send us home, uncork
At our ease a spirit whose sheer, lingering immediacy
Was smoke on the tongue for anyone who ever
Told us once we shouldn't have to be told twice.

Jordan Smith

A BAMBOO FLY ROD FROM
MY FATHER-IN-LAW'S BARN

Not a collector's item, not a Payne or Leonard, no lesson
In the power of proper names properly placed, not an inheritance
Of more value than it's worth in use, this six-weight, chrome-
Feruled, hardware store fly rod was made in the factory
An hour south of here, a decent job of work for the local trade,
Here where the hills start their sharp ascent towards mountains,
But it's still too much farm country for tourists, and the streams
Are small and brushy, the rocks slick with moss, and one slip
And you take a spill, your reel's lost in a sinkhole, rod tip
Shattered. I thought I'd hang it on the wall or just
Set in somewhere safe in the cellar, in that same tattered
Green cloth case, but I remember my friend, before
He'd lost one marriage and found another country, wading
In khakis and old sneakers, up to his belt in the current, his tackle
Buttoned into one shirt pocket, no vest or hat, his line
Singing out as he headed for deeper, faster currents, his cheap
Fly rod like a baton summoning the praise of light on water, and so
In honor of his recklessness, which was only pleasure, I think it's time
To string this one up, tie on a pattern from that guy in Rock City Falls
Who doesn't even name his flies, just says they work as well
As anything else on those uncatchable trout of early spring,
So taut in bright chaos of reflection and refraction, so
Fleet, so fleeting these humble instruments of joy.

– from *The Names of Things Are Leaving* (University of Tampa Press, 2005)

Jordan Smith

THE PLEASING PROSPECT

...in the exquisite clarity, every detail is visible
GEORGE MOORE, on Ashford Castle

Of the half-barbaric lough beyond the barbered lawn,
Is someone's hand at work, at welcome, and you might think
The author had this particular light of mind in mind: after
A morning's drizzle and attendant mists and a walk
From the abbey's gravestones, that the clouds would shift
Enough dull gravity to allow (this is a landscape that invites
Another century's allegory) hope to imbue the picturesque
With... Well, you can imagine for yourself the grandiosely
Detailed painting, an academician's folderol, failed but
Unfailingly polite, retired from salon to dusty country house
Wall, and left for our gently condescending pleasure
Before the server brings the bill. On the Shannon bus,
There was a drug deal going down in the back seat,
Three boys making sure we all knew to the penny
What ecstasy costs, and so much for all those postcard
Views, until we dropped them at the depot lot by a gas station.
And if I thought then how traveling seems to get you exactly
Nowhere, now let's raise a glass in this wood paneled room
To wishful thinking, while all that sublime pity and terror
Slides into abeyance, such a good word for our tenancy
Of expectation in a world that is always someone else's estate,
And if by some accident or oversight or slight deceit
We got in that door, we might as well take the seat they offer
And all we never but the pleasing prospect could afford.

Edward Boyne

TRIBE

When they found themselves on the new ground,
the tribe felt astray, like they had no right or claim
to be caught there. The marks and odours of the fond past
were absent, just a worrying plastered freshness
and an unhindered winter-chill breeze.

There were no signs of usual purpose,
labour on boats or barrels, no cooper's aprons,
no docker's haunts, granite steps, sawdust pubs,
no lorry-scutting, no animal gangs.
Blackened teeth were outlawed. A charwoman
was a 'cleaner' and corpses were laid out by nurses.
No smell of hops or putrid river, no tuggers,
fancy-women, kip houses, coal boats, stone bruises,
slop buckets.
Everything new was a form of no.
It was all to happen like a sink draining,
no questions asked, no answers given.
Go.

There were still and shady trees, and if no trees
there were fields, or 'meadows' as was said
in the new language. The suddenly original children
were to have childhoods, their own clean bed
raised on legs off the floor and no toil intended.
Books were forced in the new doors,
to be read and re-read. At times a studious quiet descended
that was never heard before, tight as a judge.
Soon there was a grammar imposed on breathing itself
on the raised voice and shiny accents, softer melodies
masking all the rough bliss that went before.

There were signs of livestock, dark forms,
stragglers, keeping shyly to the distance.
The tribe didn't know the names of these breeds,
neither had the animals seen the tribe's like,
and soon without ceremony or comment
the cattle and other beasts vanished
as the massed roofs pushed westwards,
trailing car-parks and shopping centres,
motorists, customers.

Theo Dorgan

THE ANGEL OF DAYS

to Eugene Lambert

And what did you do on earth?

I did my work.

I went at it all wide-eyed,
with a steady heart.
I reared strong sons and daughters,
I mastered my craft.

And what was the best of it?

Loving, and being loved.

I pity God, who never walked home by night
or drove the length of Ireland in the rain,
or came in from the workshop
with a new story, sawdust and glue on his hands,
to Mai in the full house—such a welcome I had!

And what would you have changed?

Nothing. Not one blessed thing.

I loved my world—
the hush when a story started up,
watching my hands at work,
children, their laughter.
I never minded the black days—
storms will blow over, it's their nature.

And what will you do now?

It's been a long road, I might have a rest.
I might do a small bit of work.

Ailbhe Slevin

THE FAIRY MIDWIFE: A RETELLING

The knock, when it came after midnight, was sharp and imperious. The widow was not disturbed by the sound or the lateness of the hour. She was often called upon at strange times to assist some young mother in her confinement. A kindly soul, with a great knowledge of herbs and their uses, she was trusted by all in the parish.

But the man at her door was not of the parish. Pulling her shawl a little more closely around her body, the widow looked up at the tall stranger, and saw fear and anxiety in his handsome face. She spoke first.

'Your wife, Sir? She needs me?'

He nodded gratefully and gestured towards his horse, a fine white stallion standing quietly by the road. The widow concealed her surprise; this man was most definitely not from these parts, and a gentleman at that. Why had he called at the door of a lowly rural midwife when he must surely have the finest doctors in the land at his command? She allowed him to lift her onto the horse with him and asked no questions.

They travelled at speed across the land, seeming to cover great distances in very little time. Though she could barely make out the fields which flew by so swiftly, the widow realised that she was already a long way from home. The stranger was silent, his face set against the wind, betraying none of his thoughts but his desire to complete the journey with all haste.

They had reached their destination. The stranger brought his horse to a halt and lifted the widow down to the ground. She stared incredulous at the grand house before them, the like of which she had never seen or even heard tell of in the whole province. Almost a castle, it rose in elegant proportions from the hill, the faintest of mists hanging around its parapets.

The stranger opened the great door and bade her enter. The grandeur and beauty of the exterior kept its promise; the widow saw a vast hall with an imposing staircase of white marble at the centre of it, and every kind of richness all around. She followed her host wordlessly to a room upstairs where she found his wife, a beautiful lady, lying in a tapestry bed in great distress. Seeing the pale frightened face of the lady, the widow forgot all the grandness around her and thought only of making her comfortable. For in spite of her obvious wealth and status, she was just like all the other girls she helped through their labours over the years.

It was not long before the widow went to find the husband to tell him that his wife had safely delivered a fine boy, dark haired like his father, bright eyed like his mother. Both parents were profuse in their thanks, and the widow watched the new family with a quiet joy in her heart.

A short time later, the husband approached the widow and told her he had one more request to make of her. Placing a small vial of ointment in her hand he said:

'Anoint the eyes of the child with this ointment. But take care: do not put it near your own eyes, lest you see as you should not'.

The widow was full of questions, but as was her way, she remained silent. She did as she was told and anointed the eyes of the sleeping infant with the fine, silvery ointment, wondering all the time.

When it was time to leave she went to bid farewell to mother and child, barely stifling a yawn, for day was breaking and she had not yet seen her own bed. Rubbing her eyes with tiredness, she realised too late that traces of the ointment still clung to one finger and before she knew it she had anointed her left eye.

And from that eye, she now saw a very different scene. Gone was the beautiful house with its marble staircase and fine furnishings; instead she stood in a filthy hovel with a rough earth floor. The mother and her baby lay not on a luxurious bed but on and old straw pallet, with a threadbare horse blanket for covering, and a hole in the roof letting the rain in. When she closed her left eye she saw the opulence restored, and with both eyes open the sight was neither one thing nor the other; now majestic, now humble, until her head began to spin. But as always, the widow knew that now more than ever she must hold her peace, and said nothing.

She took her leave of mother and child with a blessing, and allowed the husband to lift her on to his horse, even though she now saw that it was no horse at all but an old plank of wood. Keeping her eyes tight shut, they hurtled towards her home, and after a hasty goodbye, the widow closed her door behind her with great relief.

The weeks that followed were a both a wonder and a torment. Two worlds the widow saw, her own from her right eye and the other from her left. Some of the sights were beautiful and dreamlike, others were terrible to behold. In fleeting glances, she met people the like of which she had never known in her own world. They took her by the hand and bid her join in their games, showing her glimpsing visions that made her old heart race. But in time she cursed her dual sight, for she was exhausted and it became impossible to get any work done, until she began to think that perhaps there were some things better left unseen, no matter how wonderful.

It was one day at the market when she saw the father of the baby she had delivered to the fine lady that night when it all began. When she saluted him and asked after the health of his wife and son, he started in amazement, and then peered closely into her face.

'Can you see me?' he said to her and when she replied that she could he asked 'Which eye?'

It was not without some relief that she explained that she saw him with her left eye only, and how she had rubbed in the ointment by mistake, for she had been afraid to tell anyone what had happened in case they thought her mad. He spoke again:

'There are those of my kind who would blind you for this. But you showed every kindness to my wife, and for that I will partly spare you. The sight, however, I must take back'.

With that, he blew into her left eye and disappeared, taking with him all signs of the other world to which she had been a witness, as well as every bit of light and vision from that same blighted eye. All she saw now with the one good eye the gentleman had left her with was the coming and going of the marketplace, as ordinary a sight as any.

And if, on long winter nights, she ever had a small bit of longing for the beauty she had once spied in that other world, she dismissed it readily enough. For she was a sensible sort of woman and she knew as well as anyone that there are some things better left unseen, no matter how wonderful.

Eamon Grennan

OWL LIGHT

Standing vigil on sea-verge at Letterfrack inlet the heron's a pale mist-grey
      and faint translucence among ambers and blacks of sea-wrack while plovers
bescreech the rainswept tide by Glassillaun where a family of terns hover
      before plunging as white projectiles into the indigo and avocado water
and the young cry out as they learn to dive for their lives and carry their tribe
      into farther millennia while wind-driven spongy rain-rags are shawling
Leitir Hill where a drenched cow is bellowing and then it's evening and Venus
      is a small radiance simmering in the west under clouds daubed amber
peach and slate-grey and then the little things kick in with child-bleatings of
      bare lambs on the mountain whose dirt-shredded shearings are left to rot
in barns beside which the brown flicker of a chaffinch can be seen between
      ash branches while all the while Dürer's owl looks down on the man
at his writing table and *Here* he says (the owl says) *one way or the other*
      by clockface or by starlight here we are.

Eamon Grennan

THE POLITICS OF PRIMO MAGGIO

Now a singing cardinal gives its signal blessing to this May Day morning
  in which the republic of grass and the roused democracy of weeds
and all the contracts earth can agree with the communist intrigues of air
  proclaim a hopeful truce a truthful expansion of what's possible
into the very realm of the actual—a natural colonizing by its own best interests
  of the ever-ground we stand on to quicken to flourish to continue
and all other such infinitives of the here and now we here now live by.

Eamon Grennan

TOUCHING HERACLITUS

The soiled-socks under-the-oxter sex-in-a-jam-factory smell of leaf-rot swaddling air
      is a match maybe for the sobering eye-world of leathery browns of the last leaves
fallen or fixed still to twigs and branches (oak sycamore maple) on a day of cloud
      patched with blue tatters while snow and cold in the forecast must break the spell
of unseasonable Fall weather and again he hears *potamoisi toisin autoisin* and knows
      (he'll step in he'll feel it) that everything flows that stays what it was and (stepped in)
he'll feel-hear the firestream kissing—*listen!*—the ashtree's reluctant heartwood.

Susan Lanigan

INFINITE LOOP

The tenor is on his way home when the train breaks down. It stops at Grand Canal Dock station and refuses to start. The lights go out in the carriage and a half-heard announcement asks people in the train to get out onto the platform and wait. Eventually they all obey.

He is tired. All afternoon he has been giving singing lessons in the south Dublin suburbs and the pupils seem more recalcitrant than usual, more resistant to improvement. Their mothers have sent them to him, of course, on account of his reputation. Good enough to teach, not so good that his ego might outshine theirs.

The shoppers complain and shiver as carols blare through speakers onto the street below. Christmas, making its business known throughout the city whether people want it to or not. On impulse, the tenor leaves the station, even though he has three more stops to go before a twenty-minute walk to his apartment in Glasnevin. He hates waiting.

As he passes through newly-installed automatic gates at Grand Canal Dock station, he loops his scarf ever more tightly about his neck. He, more than others, cannot afford to let the raw, wet slap of the wind get into his throat and lungs. This time of year is a busy one for him.

Heading down for the docks, he passes the new theatre, the offices around it lit up like chessboards, the long, stone seats with green strip lighting, the spotlights set in the ground, at last making his way over to a group of luminous, red poles bent at angles like miniature towers of Pisa. Tiny droplets of rain brush his cheek. He coughs—and in the pause following that cough he hears someone singing.

She is standing at the water's edge, coatless with long dark hair. The melody he can divine immediately: it is the Dance of the Maidens from Alexander Borodin's opera *Prince Igor*, the alto line beginning "There beneath the burning sky". But she is not singing in Russian.

"...for I is nothing, I is less than end, I plus plus, open bracket, end plus plus, and close it again..."

He does not know what she means. He can, however, tell that her voice is untrained, a little weak around the higher notes, but tuneful enough. She sways from side to side as she sings, as if in a trance. As he stands there watching, her skirt moves a little in the breeze and he sees, with a thrill of intimate shock, that she is barefoot. Barefoot, in the middle of December! Scuffed black pumps, the kind worn to work by millions, are lined up a few feet away, as if waiting to walk into the water by themselves.

Here is where he should tap her on the shoulder and say "Excuse me, is everything all right?" But for all his geniality at a concert's end, his shaking of everyone's hand after a demanding performance—for all that, he is now overcome with a shyness that breaks across him like a warm wave. Here, out in the open, he is a man well into middle age, a man not so forward, not so courageous. His intent might be misconstrued. There might be trouble.

So he listens from a distance as she repeats her melody, not interrupting until she reaches the bar before "I is nothing." Then he comes in with his line, leading into the next verse. It is much easier, he finds, to interrupt a stranger when one is singing rather than speaking. His voice, trained and in full power, stops her almost instantly. She turns around and watches him as he sings the rest:

As we sang together, languid breezes cooled us, there the cloud-capped mountains sailed above the silver sea...

"Who are you?" she says when he comes to a stop. In the garish light of one of the nearby tubes, he can see that she is dark-skinned, though she sings and speaks with an Irish accent. She looks about twenty-five.

"Someone who likes Borodin," he says.

She pulls a cardigan around her. "Do you know how he died?" she asks.

"Who? Borodin?"

She nods.

"Here, you're cold, take my coat." For all his worry about catching a chill a few moments ago, he is now putting his coat around her shoulders, its wool-fibre thickness helping to keep his wary hands at a distance. Even so, she still hunches her shoulders, her entire body contracting in that one movement as she ducks from him. But she puts her arms in the holes.

"He was dancing at a party," she says, "and his heart exploded. Just like that, in the middle of a dance. His aorta just burst. He was only fifty-one."

"I'm fifty-five." He has no idea why he just said that. She says nothing, shrinking into that coat, shivering more with it on than off. Although he is not a large man, the coat is still far too big for her. He is reminded of a poem

47

by Ezra Pound, part of a collection of poetry books on his bookshelf. "Portrait d'une Femme," he thinks it's called. He will have to go back and check later. But why is she here? She is obviously distressed about something, to be barefoot in that state and rambling about Borodin, the poor child.

"You're wrong, you know," he says, deciding to comfort her.

"What about?"

"Being less than zero. You're not. You're worth so much more. Time will show you, I promise."

He means to impart experience to her youth, but it comes out all wrong. His voice, for a start, too high-pitched and boyish—an annoying professional hazard—and the words themselves, lacking gravitas. From the look on her face, he has got something wrong. She stares at him for a while and then starts to laugh as he struggles to guess his error. Her laugh is a high-pitched breathy ha-ha that seems out of kilter with her singing voice.

"It's C++ code," she explains. "I was reciting a FOR loop and putting it to music. 'I' isn't me, it's a variable whose value increases as I go around the loop. It starts off being zero and each iteration means it goes up one in value. "Plus-plus" means plus one. It was something bothering me at work last week."

He looks at her quizzically.

"I'm a programmer. C++ is the language I write code in." She allows herself a little smile, the corners of her mouth turning up.

"A programmer!" he echoes, trying to conceal his surprise. The wind is beginning to bite; he can feel his shirt billowing against his skin. He would never have guessed, not in a million years, what she did for a living. He did not grow up in a time where girls went near machines, even though heaven knows it is commonplace enough now.

"Yes, I'm a geek," she says, her smile now a fully-fledged grin, "and what do you do?"

"I sing."

"For a living?" She is as surprised as he, looking at him in disbelief.

"It's been known to happen," he says, slightly affronted. "I'm a member of the Aula Cantata."

"I thought you were a banker. You look like one."

He decides to ignore that comment. "Did you come here from work?" He glances at her shoes once more.

She looks at the ground, embarrassed at where his eyes have wandered. "They fired me this morning. Said they wanted to move forward. They meant me to move forward out of their office and never come back. Ever since then

I've been walking round in circles. I don't know where I am. I don't know who I am." Her voice cracks at that point and she swallows quickly, half-turning away from him.

"Please go on," he says gently.

Although he is a talkative man, he knows when to be patient. Without interrupting, he listens as she tells him about her roommates giving her the "talk." They want her out before the end of the week. They are angry at her, it seems, for taking a man into her room, a one-night stand rather than a regular, live-in boyfriend. He recognises the type of woman she is talking about. The mother of the girl he almost married thirty-three years ago treated him the same way. He would not do as a suitor for Eileen Fennell; he was too eccentric, too open. Too Protestant, though she never said it in so many words. Strange, that something so long ago should stir up such anger in him. He met Eileen Fennell again a few months back, on Grafton Street, for the first time in years. Like him she has aged and thickened, but the light in her eyes was still there when they met. Eileen Corless, she is now. He fielded her questions, joking about his eternal bachelor status, enquiring about her husband and family. She was up for a hospital appointment. Tests, she said. The many shopping bags she carried made him suspect that her husband and children knew nothing of the true purpose of her trip and that the results were potentially more serious than she was letting on. The bags were just a decoy. They stood in the flow of pedestrian traffic making small talk—each, he suspected, pitying the other's fate—before walking away.

"I suppose you'll judge me too."

The girl is addressing him, her chin pointed defiantly upwards.

I have wasted my life, he thinks, and the force of the thought almost knocks him backwards. He is trembling now, shivering in his shirt; the pretence of being cold helps mask his inner turmoil. He hopes so, anyway.

"Those women did you wrong," he says, finding his voice at last, "because they were afraid of you. Most people don't tolerate people like you and me. We have to make do the best we can. Keep going around the loop, as it were." He smiles at her and throws a few notes in the air, going up from middle C to G and back down again. "Ah—ah—ah—ah—*ah*—ah—ah—ah—*ah*—"

"Stop!" she cries.

"You're not the only one who can do infinite loops, my darling. I could sing this all night."

"Please don't—even if it is lovely."

There is a pause. He can tell she does not want to go home; for his part, he does not want to sound too eager to keep her there. No-one is waiting for him in that demure, lifeless terrace in Glasnevin, no-one apart from Ezra Pound.

"I'd better go," she says, breaking the impasse, "it was nice to meet you." She walks up beside him and whispers in his ear. "I was thinking of jumping. It's shallow though. I can't even get that right."

Then she puts her palm on the small of his back, between his shoulder blades. His shirt fabric is thin; he can feel the warmth of her hand pressing that tender spot, very gently, just for a few seconds, a benediction. He sighs lightly, involuntarily, at her touch.

She lifts her hand and drops his coat at his feet. "Goodbye," she says, walking away quickly. Now her step is decisive. Watching her, he sees that she no longer sways from side to side. He does not move or speak while she is still in his vision, waiting until her shape gets smaller and smaller in the distance until it disappears into the dark.

*

That night, the tenor walks the whole way from Grand Canal Dock to his apartment in Glasnevin. When he finally lets himself in, his rooms are shrouded in darkness, no sound to be heard but the hum of the fridge. He imagines the girl arriving at her rented place for her last few days, inching quietly into her bedroom as the other girls watch soaps on the television and throw their weight around the kitchen, having made it clear to her that she is there only on sufferance.

Without turning on the light, he lifts the piano lid and plays a chord, an augmented fourth. Ouch. Then he begins to sing. He does not know what it is, or how loud he will be. He doesn't care if neighbours complain. Just for once he will love the song once more, not think of the money or lost opportunities or an uncertain future. No expectations: there is not much future left anyway, certain or otherwise.

He is unaware that fingers, their bitten nails pale against dark skin, are typing "Aula Cantata" into an internet search engine in a laptop in a poky third bedroom in a southside Dublin flat. Nor does he imagine that a quick glance at the website is all that is needed to ascertain his name; that a search on his name in turn elicits his e-mail address and phone number, left carelessly around the place like small change. No, he does not yet know what is to come. But tonight, he sings for love. That is all that matters.

Christian Wallace

MUSIC IN THE CHURCH

With eyes shut, I sense spirits passing around my pew.
A dark-haired girl fingers a fiddle on the stone stage.
The minister joins her, his lips to the flute
are shaped for sounds not unlike a sermon.
Bashful in his plain clothes, his feet tap time
in sandals like Christ might have worn
if a Dunne's Store stood near the Mount.
He speaks between sets: the places where each tune
first came to flute or fiddle, the counties of Ireland
spoken of as individual, storied nations.
The flash from a camera pulls at the pane
of stained glass from outside the church—the church
increasingly curious to agnostic tourists.
The minister ignores the flash,
his eyebrows raised to his baldness in concentration.
Safe now in his own sacred stronghold, he shifts
tempo and tone, plays a tune for the Ulster Scots
who marched in their own strange time to war.
I remember the Connacht Ranger, dead at twenty-nine,
his plaque among the others on the church walls.
Outside the sliding notes, I feel the jaws of history
swallowing the dead Ranger and Ulster Scots.
Their deaths, noble or not, marked only by a bit of brass
and a trad tune echoing in the starving belly of a church.

Christian Wallace

THE DAY AFTER THANKSGIVING

I had just passed Sterling City. If I went much further
there would be no chance of finding the right tumbleweed
to bring back to San Marcos, to string with lights and hang
green and red ornaments from the weaving brittle limbs.
I scanned the sides of the road until I saw one, and
pulled onto the shoulder. It was big, looked intact, perfect.
My dog, Loretta, followed me up the highway to the dead bush
caught against the barbed-wire fence. She noticed the deer first.
One hoof was twisted between strands of the wire fencing.
A tuft of hair clung to the hoof before sun-bleached bone
stabbed the November sky. The rest of her—spinal cord,
hip bone, ribs, the skull—lay scattered along the fenceline.
I imagined her struggling to free the hoof. She might have
died of thirst or a combination of heat and exhaustion.
More likely the coyotes found her and consumed her,
stripped the bones of flesh still warmed by her beating heart.
My dog sniffed at the hoof. I wondered if the smell of death
still lingered or had it dried like blood in the sun?
I put the tumbleweed in the truck-bed,
used sun-rotted bungees to strap it down.
Four more hours and still a hundred miles from home.
I took a dirt road to the West Sweden Cemetery,
stopped to let Loretta run. The gate was unlocked.
The polyester flowers left on the graves were faded.
No one had been buried there for years,
but the lawn was neatly trimmed and no plastic bags stuck
in the mesquite trees around the place. There was nothing
beyond but pastures of dead grass and rows and rows
of tilled red dirt sometimes studded with cotton.

There were no windmills, no cattle. There was no water
inside the earth. I thought about the people beneath me.
Most were probably skeletons still dressed
in their Sunday best: dark suits, flower-patterned dresses.
Against the barbed-wire fence on the west end, a cross
rose slanted from the ground as if it had grown
searching for the sun. A name was etched into the stone.
My birthday was beneath it—a date of death, too.
I called for Loretta, checked the tumbleweed,
watched the cigarette smoke slip out the open window.
As I drove further: the sky darkening.

Val Nolan

A DESCRIPTIVE LIST OF THE PAPERS OF A. ANNLLOV

Reference code:	X42
Title:	The Papers of A. Annllov
Date(s):	c.1907–1909
Extent:	1 box
Location:	James Hardiman Library, NUIG

BIOGRAPHICAL CONTEXT: Little is known about Alexander Annllov, a Russian émigré who joined the Abbey Theatre as a rigger and carpenter in 1907. Having first worked in a succession of small London playhouses, Annllov eventually made his way to Dublin where his technical skill and experience proved of value to the Abbey. During his three years with the company, Annllov amassed a small collection of original documents by and relating to key figures in the theatre. It is believed he acquired this material unofficially, retrieving much of it from waste paper baskets and dustbins.

IMMEDIATE SOURCE OF ACQUISITION OR TRANSFER: The twenty-one items of this collection were deposited by Mr. Annllov's grand-nephew in September 2003.

SYSTEM OF ARRANGEMENT: Given their curious nature, as well as the unlikely narrative they present, the decision has been made to present this material chronologically.

X42/1   SCOPE AND CONTENT: Pencil sketch (artist unknown) showing WB Yeats and JM Synge. The image is notable for the atypical presentation of its subjects, Yeats shown with feet resting on his desk, clad in what appear to be cowboy boots. Beside him is Synge, gaunt, with a glass in his hand and a worried look upon his face. Though difficult to tell from the sketch, the books surrounding them appear to contain occult symbols.
    DATE: 2nd February 1909.

X42/2   SCOPE AND CONTENT: Typescript list of readings compiled by WB Yeats, possibly related to a Creative Writing course he delivered. Includes stories by Sheridan Le Fanu, George Moore, and Yeats himself. Verso contains a handwritten fragment of 'The Fascination of What's Difficult'.

DATE: 10th February 1909.

X42/3   SCOPE AND CONTENT: Handwritten draft of JM Synge's *Deirdre of the Sorrows* beginning 'There are lonesome days and bad nights in this place like any other...'. Ring-shaped stains on the paper are characteristic of red wine spillages. Handwritten notes on the verso of page four record observations about death and dying. Paginated pp. 4–39.

DATE: 14th February 1909.

X42/4   SCOPE AND CONTENT: Handwritten letter to WB Yeats from an individual identified as 'A.C.'. The writer describes his desire to travel to Ireland and enlist Yeats's assistance in 'unearthing the elemental powers of the world'; also acknowledges the surprising nature of this request given their 'cordial hatred' for one another. The correspondent writes that 'I have recently cast a horoscope for you and the projections are, in the main, quite favourable. What we discover might even help your friend with his [*word indecipherable*]. It certainly would be a shame if anything happened to him'. Letter is written on paper with a 'Cecil Hotel, London' heading.

DATE: 20th February 1909, postmarked 22nd February 1909.

X42/5   SCOPE AND CONTENT: Handwritten receipt from a doctor's surgery in Mount Pleasant Square, Dublin. Made out to JM Synge.

DATE: 23rd February 1909.

X42/6   SCOPE AND CONTENT: Handwritten draft of a letter from WB Yeats. Begins 'My dear Frater Perdurabo: I did not expect to hear from you again though, as I recall, you do have old documents which I know have caused you endless trouble. Am I to presume that you have now divined some ancient knowledge from them? Or at least you have convinced yourself that you have? If so be warned, the site which your wretched hand describes is probably the most consecrated spot in Ireland. I would not have you or any of your proxies mine it for naught but evidence of your astounding ignorance. Neither shall I help you in your quest, for to do so would contradict all I have ever done or thought. There is vulgarity to your suggestion, plenty of it, but worse—what you propose is downright madness. You are not wanted on these shores and I will not allow you the means to gain control over the conscience of many. As to our past quarrels, these matters are of course private and I expect them to remain as such.' This draft displays considerable amendments and corrections. It has no correlation amongst Yeats's *Collected Letters*.

DATE: 1st March 1909.

X42/7   SCOPE AND CONTENT: Typescript draft of JM Synge's *Deirdre of the Sorrows* containing the opening section of Act II. The verso of page forty-five displays what appears to be a short comment in Synge's hand. Begins 'The electrical and energetic therapies pioneered on the continent may yet hold some hope. I have had promising correspondence from several of the doctors involved however the widespread implementation of their work is obviously some years away. What I wouldn't give to recreate their progress here in Ireland...' Paginated pp. 43-61. Missing page 49.

DATE: 15th March 1909.

X42/8   SCOPE AND CONTENT: Newspaper clipping from a gossip column noting the arrival in Dublin of 'the wickedest man in the world'. Said individual 'has been enquiring around town as to the whereabouts of a certain Irish poet. No doubt he seeks a rematch after their last encounter, the "Battle of Blythe Road" some years ago in London. Perhaps we might suggest he take in a show at the Abbey?'

DATE: 16th March 1909.

X42/9   SCOPE AND CONTENT: Fragment of a ticket stub from British and Irish Steampacket Company. Ticket belonged to an individual named Crowley.

DATE: 16th March 1909.

X42/10 SCOPE AND CONTENT: Typewritten letter from the *Proceedings of the American Society for Psychical Research* (St. Louis, Missouri) addressed to DEDI (Demon Est Deus Inversus i.e. WB Yeats). Letter is a reply to Yeats's request for information on 'marshalling spiritual forces to repel undesirable magical influences'. Enclosed is a copy of the Society's guidelines on the matter: 'Ritual Q, Part IV, containing 'symbolism of admission to Neophyte Grade' as well as 'Closing Oration'. Paginated pp. 1-14.

DATE: 18th March 1909.

X42/11 SCOPE AND CONTENT: Letter from Jean Duchamp, Hôtel Corneille at 5, Rue Corneille, Paris. Addressed to JM Synge. The sender expresses her regret that John Synge had to undergo further treatment for cancer and that she and her husband hope to meet with Synge on their next visit to Dublin. No signature; last page probably missing. Enclosed are newspaper clippings from French daily papers which detail ongoing oncological experiments involving electromagnetic waves.

DATE: 18th March 1909.

X42/12 SCOPE AND CONTENT: Writing book given to WB Yeats by Lady Gregory in March 1909. At head of 1st leaf: 'Private'. On verso of leaf one: letter (fragment) to WB Yeats from Lady Gregory. Begins 'Found this on The Strand and thought it quite your style.' Pages two and three contain Yeats's observations about JM Synge, including how his illness is affecting his behaviour and his writing. Begins 'Synge is very ill now and cannot be asked about matters of business. He is perhaps dying. Nothing is known with any certainty as the doctors do not understand the nature of the growth or whether it is the coming again of that which first made him ill. He was very week [sic] and pale when I saw him today, and he finds any conversation about literature too exciting. His hatred of death is obvious and he betrays all the desperations and temptations a man cannot fail but show in the course of his final days.' Further pages contain astrological material, accounts of séances, Tarot matter, and reference to 'the great gold box of the Israelites'.

DATE: 19th March 1909.

X42/13 SCOPE AND CONTENT: Fragment of a handwritten letter to JM Synge from an unidentified correspondent. Begins '…so you understand my predicament and will, I hope, give real consideration to my suggestion. With your assistance, the Demon might be more easily persuaded. Moreover, there are the benefits to you which we discussed, the incredible energies to be harnessed which [*words indecipherable*] you.' First and last pages missing.

DATE: 19th March 1909.

X42/14 SCOPE AND CONTENT: Pages torn from the *Journal of the Royal Society of Antiquities of Ireland*. Pages contain two articles: Murphy, Denis and Westropp, Thomas J. 'Notes on the Antiquities of Tara', *JRSAI* Vol. XXIV (1894), pp. 232-242 and O'Reilly, DJ. 'An Account of Excavations at the Hill of Tara Conducted by the British-Israel Association, 1899-1902', *JRSAI*, Vol. XXXIII (1903), pp. 77-92. Both articles have been heavily annotated by WB Yeats. Begins 'It is almost the equinox and, should my calculations be correct, the opening of the window Perdurabo seeks'. Handwritten notes continue with many calculations based on astrological formulae. One comment, towards the end of the O'Reilly article, acknowledges Yeats's defacement of holdings from the library of the Dublin Museum of Science and Art: 'It seemed too dangerous to leave these where I found them, least they fall into unscrupulous hands. No, they are safer with me or—like most human knowledge—safer again if they are lost forever.'

DATE: 20th March 1909.

X42/15 SCOPE AND CONTENT: Handwritten letter from Maude Gonne to WB Yeats. Begins 'The attic here is a frightful place but I have endured the indignity of mouseshit and low beams to retrieve this for you. The rite itself is basic enough, though therein lies the beauty of it all: young Aleister will have steeled himself for a replay of Blythe Road and will thus have left himself vulnerable to a slew of lesser magiks.' Enclosed: typewritten copy of a 'Portal Ritual' as issued to 'those who are Zelator Adeptus Minor and have finished their training in Magical Weapons'. Stapled to Golden Dawn ownership slip and dated 20th December 1896. Considerable annotations by Maude Gonne and WB Yeats. Paginated pp. 1-20.

DATE: 20th March 1909 (covering letter).

X42/16 SCOPE AND CONTENT: Seven leaves of hand-drawn sketches by WB Yeats. Annotations identify these pages as attempts to solve the 'Great Irish-Hebraic-cryptogramic hieroglyph'. The obverse of four sheets display WB Yeats's handwritten notes on inscriptions of Celtic artefacts from the Royal Irish

Academy (including diagrams on two sheets). Begins 'A sacrifice is required, though whether the door is locked or unlocked will all depend on he who turns the key'. There follows, on the final page, Yeats's observations about those closest to him: Begins 'The question of character has never been of greater import…'

DATE: 21st March 1909.

X42/17 SCOPE AND CONTENT: Handwritten note from JM Synge on a 'With Compliments' slip displaying the Abbey Theatre logo: 'To whoever may find this, it would seem that I have a choice to make. One which no doubt would appear fantastikal to you if I explained it but one which is altogether real. Times are changing—the *world* is changing—and I do not have a script for how this all turns out. I fear there will be no tidy ending for me yet; it would be foolish to believe otherwise. In the event that I do not return I would ask whoever reads this note to dispose of all my correspondence. Fire would be the best.'

DATE: 22nd March 1909.

X42/18 SCOPE AND CONTENT: Newspaper clipping of a gossip column noting Yeats and Synge's departure from Dublin. Begins 'The Abbey's erstwhile duo were up early for a change in order to catch a motorcoach for County Meath this morning. Asked if his journey had anything to do with recent archaeological excavations at the Hill of Tara, the esoterically-inclined Mr. Yeats questioned this reporter's knowledge, appearance, parentage, and penmanship. It would seem that the man who dreamed of faeryland would do best to get more than four hours sleep! And yet, alongside the whiskey-health of the poet's rosy cheeks, Mr. Synge's shook countenance could not be more apparent. While many have attributed this to recent talk of disagreements between the pair, it seems that rumours of the playwright's illness are not exaggerated. Just imagine the catcalls from the cheap seats if we've lost him surely.'

DATE: 23rd March 1909.

X42/19 SCOPE AND CONTENT: Carbon of a typewritten letter to the Navan Constabulary from landlord Gustavus Villiers Briscoe. Briscoe, then owner of the land on which the Hill of Tara complex is sited, complains about trespasses conducted by WB Yeats, JM Synge, and an unnamed third party: 'On the night of 24th March 1909 I was woken by the sounds of scuffles and explosions occurring on my land. Looking from the window I saw strange colours emanating from the hilltop and I heard the sound of screaming, screeching, and Latin incantation. Arming myself with my fowling piece, I recruited a number of nearby tenants to help me investigate. Ascending towards the commotion, we made no more than a third of the summit before our way was blocked by an imperceptible wall. It was unlike anything I have ever seen, a blue glimmer of the aether past which we could not proceed. Having sent my tenants around the hill I can confirm that this invisible barrier completely enclosed the antiquities and the three individuals within. Two of these were recognisable to me from the newspapers as WB Yeats and JM Synge of the Abbey Theatre. The third I did not know. Evidently Yeats and the mystery figure were engaged in a duel of some sort. I witnessed multiple muzzle flashes but without any evidence of pistols in their hands. Hits were clearly scored on either side however neither man fell until the end. As this occurred, Mr. Synge busied himself in the muck, as is his way. He appeared to be excavating something from my land while, overhead, a dusty golden tumult whirled throughout the air. The light, when it came, was blinding. It appeared to emerge from underneath the earth, from Mr. Synge's position, and it lit the hillside like the sun itself. At this, Mr. Yeats and his adversary both collapsed. There was a roar then too, a sound so terrible that I thought the world was breaking open. I do not know how long it lasted but when my estate had once again lapsed into silent darkness only Mr. Yeats remained. Pushing through the now-weakened barrier, my men and I attempted to apprehend him but he slunk away into wooded ground before we were within reach. Given the disruption caused to myself and my livestock by these events, I would see Mr. Yeats charged with unlawful trespass and criminal damage. I would also question his role in the true fate of Mr. Synge.'

Also enclosed: an enquiry from the Navan Constabulary about Yeats's whereabouts on March 24th. In particular, Yeats is requested to clarify if he has any knowledge of 'disturbed earthworks, an intense auroral display, and the lingering phenomena of spinning compass needles suggestive of unexplained and unlicensed electromagnetic activity'.

DATE: 2nd April 1909.

X42/20 SCOPE AND CONTENT: Newspaper clipping headlined *Playwright Buried in Dublin*. Article describes JM Synge's funeral, though the nationalist author offers only grudging words about the deceased. Begins 'Tributes have been paid to the late John Millington Synge who was buried this week at Mount Jerome Cemetery in Harold's Cross after a closed casket ceremony. While the stated cause of death was Hodgkin's Disease, mystery still surrounds the circumstances of Mr. Synge's demise. Asked to comment, friend and colleague WB Yeats denied any impropriety and remarked that Mr. Synge was 'the only man I know who was incapable of selfish thought'.

DATE: 3rd April 1909.

X42/21 SCOPE AND CONTENT: Undated handwritten draft of section XL of WB Yeats's 'The Death of Synge: Extracts from a Diary Kept in 1909', a version of the essay which differs dramatically from the published editions. Begins 'Synge is dead and I have no near friend left. And yet, as I crossed the Abbey stage tonight I felt his gentleness and courage. I saw a shade drift against the flats like the passing of a cloud's shadow above the painted hills. It was not the face, which was impossible to see, but his movements which I recognised. Standing my empty bottle upon the boards, I approached this apparition and I knew that it was him. "Death is a poor, untidy thing," I said, but the shade only shook its head. He was done with the parade of ambition and conflict I had led him through. He was beyond all that. "Thank you," I said, for it was impossible to ignore his sacrifice. The power of the box could well have healed him, this I know, but instead he chose to make it safe and seal it off forever. I would have thought it his end only now I see his spirit wander through the backdrops of the camp near Emain and I know that he lives on within his work: textual consciousness, a rebirth as something greater than himself. To call him forth again we must but read his words aloud like any invocation. Writing, yes; in the end it is the one true magic we possess.'

Available to all bona fide researchers, this collection is subject to the usual conditions of access governing consultation of archival material in this institution.

Guinn Batten

BAGGAGE

The freight of dreams
shifts in passage.

The train I board
on my 35th birthday
departs as the daughter
I did not have
arrives, no time to spare.
She drags behind her
(she's frail, and hurried)
the baggage that I had
thought was gone for good.

Ten or eleven, the girl
on the platform sets down
our baggage, and waves
her small white hand.
In this dream I believe
(and belief is fate)
it is now too late
to leave the moving train.

What's lost in dreams,
what's left on trains,
is what returns again,

and while not unchanged,
it remains what was not claimed.

Christian O'Reilly

HERE WE ARE AGAIN STILL

Here we are again still, commissioned by Galway City Council under the Per Cent for Art Scheme, was produced by Galway City Council, Galway Arts Centre and Decadent Theatre Company. It received its world premiere at Nun's Island Theatre, Galway, on October 27, 2009.

It was awarded an Arts Council grant under the Touring & Dissemination of Work Scheme and toured nationally in May 2011 as part of the Bealtaine Festival. The tour was a co-production between Christian O'Reilly, Joe Murphy (St John's Arts Centre, Listowel), Decadent Theatre and Galway Arts Centre.

CAST	*Paddy*	Eamonn Hunt
	Imelda	Bríd Ní Neachtain
	Tony	Andy Kellegher

DIRECTOR	Andrew Flynn
SET DESIGN	Owen MacCarthaigh
COSTUME DESIGN	Petra Breathnach
LIGHTING DESIGN	Adam Fitzsimons

CHARACTERS	Paddy, 60s
	Imelda, 60s
	Tony, 20s

SETTING	The action takes place on a bench outside a block of apartments.

RUNNING TIME	Act one—47 mins approx
	Act two—35 mins approx

SCENE ONE

(Night-time. Paddy sits on a bench, asleep, a cigarette burning in his fingers. Imelda enters in a dressing-gown and slippers. She's holding a glass of water.)

IMELDA   Well now. *(Paddy stirs, but doesn't wake.)*

IMELDA   Well now, I said!   *(Paddy wakes and sees Imelda.)*

IMELDA   Didn't I tell you?

PADDY   Didn't you tell me what? *(She raises the glass of water.)*

IMELDA   You're lucky I didn't throw it over you.

PADDY   If I was lucky I wouldn't have you disturbing me.

IMELDA   Which way is it you want to die? Pneumonia or up in flames?

PADDY   It's my business either way.

IMELDA   You're a fool either way.

PADDY   So I'm a fool. Aren't you more of a fool to be wasting time with me?

IMELDA   I am. I should have thrown it over you like I promised.

PADDY   Why didn't you so instead of breaking your promise?

IMELDA   I only said I'd do it if you were on fire.

PADDY   No. You said you'd do it if you caught me falling asleep with a cigarette in my hand again. Which is exactly how you caught me.

IMELDA   I'm a liar so, am I?

PADDY	Out and out.
IMELDA	That's a fine thing to call a person.
PADDY	It's the truth. People don't like the truth.
IMELDA	I could throw it over you now. For being unkind to me.
PADDY	You could. No-one would blame you.
IMELDA	You're very hard.
PADDY	Well if I am, doesn't that support my earlier point that you're a fool for wasting time with me?
IMELDA	It does. I am.
PADDY	Well why won't you go 'way so? Go to bed for yourself.
IMELDA	I can't sleep.
PADDY	Then watch television.
IMELDA	There's only so much television you can watch.
PADDY	That's true. There's only so much television you can watch and there's only so much radio you can listen to.
IMELDA	If you go to bed, I'll go to bed.
PADDY	What I do is my business, not yours.
IMELDA	It's because of you I can't sleep.
PADDY	That's not my fault.

IMELDA	It is your fault. I lie in bed thinking I'm going to have to call the fire brigade to put you out.
PADDY	I won't catch fire, Imelda, I've told you before. My clothes are too damp.
IMELDA	You'll freeze to death so.
PADDY	I won't freeze to death. It's not cold enough for that.
IMELDA	Why won't you go to bed, Paddy?
PADDY	Why won't you go to bed?
IMELDA	I do see you watching the soccer over beyond.
PADDY	Yes, the soccer. Exactly.
IMELDA	There's no soccer on this time of night.
PADDY	No. But maybe I like to get here early for the next time it's on.
IMELDA	There's no need to. You're the only one ever sits on that bench.
PADDY	You never know. Some day someone might get the notion.
IMELDA	Can you not sleep?
PADDY	Didn't you find me asleep?
IMELDA	I did.
PADDY	Don't try to put me and you in the same boat. You're the only insomniac around here.
IMELDA	So you can sleep?

PADDY	The mice won't let me.
IMELDA	Have you mice?
PADDY	Mice the size of rats and rats the size of dogs.
IMELDA	I don't believe you.
PADDY	You can believe what you like. *(Pause)*.
IMELDA	It's awful cold.
PADDY	Would you not buy yourself a new dressing-gown?
IMELDA	I wouldn't be cold only I'm out here talking to you.
PADDY	Are you going to do this every night?
IMELDA	I might. I don't know.
PADDY	What time do you go to bed?
IMELDA	Around eleven.
PADDY	How long does it take you to go to sleep?
IMELDA	Not long, I'd say. Maybe ten minutes. I don't know.
PADDY	Well from now on I'm not going to come out here till eleven minutes past eleven. *(Pause.)*
IMELDA	Would you please go to bed, Paddy?
PADDY	I'll go to bed when I want, Imelda.
IMELDA	I couldn't have it on my conscience if you died in the night.

PADDY	Stop having me on your conscience. I never asked to be on your conscience. You're certainly not on my conscience. *(Imelda is silent.)*
PADDY	You're the one who'll die of pneumonia, not me. I'm very hardy, you know. All those years I spent standing on side-lines and not once did I have a pair of warm socks, or a proper coat or a decent hat, or a scarf.
IMELDA	You always had them when I saw you.
PADDY	I'm talking about before that.
IMELDA	I didn't know you before that.
PADDY	I was hardy back then, so I was. It never leaves you, that toughness. It's in your bones.
IMELDA	Is this before you got married?
PADDY	It is.
IMELDA	But after you got married –
PADDY	I'm talking about before that.
IMELDA	Well I'm talking about after it.
PADDY	Okay, yes. There was a time I only ever went out wearing warm socks, a proper coat, a woolly hat, a woolly scarf. A time I wasn't let out without them.
IMELDA	She used be knitting them. Angela.
PADDY	She used be, yes.
IMELDA	A new one for Christmas or your birthday.

PADDY	For God's sake…
IMELDA	Least if you had them on now you'd be warm. Why don't you wear them, Paddy?
PADDY	Imelda, would you please just leave me alone? I know you mean well, but please… *(Pause.)*
IMELDA	Do you want the water?
PADDY	What for?
IMELDA	To drink. *(She hands him the glass of water. She leaves. He drinks the water. She returns with a blanket She puts it over his legs. He looks at her.)*
IMELDA	I came back for the glass. *(He hands her the glass.)*
PADDY	I know your ploy. I'll have to go inside to go to the toilet. Isn't that it?
IMELDA	I'm not that clever. *(She leaves. He removes the blanket from his lap. Lights slowly fade to black.)*

SCENE TWO

Tony is sitting on the bench. Imelda enters. She stops short when she sees Tony.

IMELDA	Who are you?
TONY	Who am I? I'm… I'm…
IMELDA	Did he give you a loan of it?
TONY	What? Who?

69

IMELDA	You think you can just sit there?
TONY	No. *(Getting up.)* I mean—sorry, I didn't know it belonged to—
IMELDA	It belongs to no-one. It's for everyone. Only no-one sits on it only Paddy.
TONY	Paddy?
IMELDA	Did he give you permission I'm asking.
TONY	No, I just… I…
IMELDA	That could be dangerous so.
TONY	I can move. I can go back inside. I didn't know.
IMELDA	No, no. Wait a minute. *(Imelda sits down. She smiles.)*
IMELDA	Thank you.
TONY	For what?
IMELDA	If you can sit here, why can't I?
TONY	I don't know.
IMELDA	Exactly. Now we'll see.
TONY	Sorry?
IMELDA	Now we'll see, I said.
TONY	Right…
IMELDA	I don't know why I didn't think of this before… .See what all the fuss is about.

TONY   Right…

IMELDA   Sit down. *(He sits.)*

IMELDA   Is it like that feeling you get in a church when you sit down?
            That you don't ever want to get up. You look around at all the
            pews and the altar and the wooden beams and the stained glass.
            I do love the stained glass. More than anything. I do love it when
            the light goes through it. When the light…

TONY   Shines?

IMELDA   Shines. Thank you. Shines through it. I do love our church. Do you?

TONY   I don't know it.

IMELDA   I don't know you, do I?

TONY   No.

IMELDA   Are you new?

TONY   Yes.

IMELDA   What number are you?

TONY   I'm just over there.

IMELDA   You're on the ground floor so.

TONY   Yes.

IMELDA   Do you get good light?

TONY   It's fine.

71

IMELDA	Are you happy there?
TONY	Yes.
IMELDA	I'm glad.
TONY	Thank you. *(Pause.)*
IMELDA	What made you decide to sit here?
TONY	I... I don't know.
IMELDA	I'm here twelve years and I never before sat here.
TONY	Why?
IMELDA	I never sit anywhere. I'm always on my feet. I don't like sitting.
TONY	Except in church? You said –
IMELDA	Except in church. Exactly. I like sitting in church. But I like lighting candles better. Do you like lighting candles?
TONY	I... I don't really go to church.
IMELDA	But you don't have candles only in churches. I have them above in my flat. I do light a scented candle if I'm after cooking a chop for myself because it gets rid of the smell, although I don't really mind the smell of a chop. I always light one if I'm after fish. Though I don't really mind that smell either. I can't really smell any more, like I used to. I miss that. Especially the flowers. Especially the roses. But other people can smell and if they come into my flat I like it to be nice for them. The odd time they come in. Yes. *(Pause. Tony takes out his cigarettes. He offers her one.)*
IMELDA	No, thank you.

TONY	Do you mind if I smoke one myself?
IMELDA	I don't. *(Tony is about to light up.)*
IMELDA	They give you lung cancer, don't they?
TONY	Some people get lung cancer.
IMELDA	Yes, people that smoke get it.
TONY	Not all smokers get it as far as I know.
IMELDA	As far as I know, they do. Or throat cancer. *(He is again about to light up.)*
IMELDA	Lung cancer or throat cancer. Or both, I suppose. *(He puts his cigarettes away.)*
TONY	I should give up.
IMELDA	You should. Why don't you?
TONY	I know.
IMELDA	You like them, I suppose.
TONY	I suppose.
IMELDA	But that's hardly a reason not to give them up, is it?
TONY	No.
IMELDA	You can like something else instead, can't you?
TONY	I suppose.

IMELDA	Something that won't kill you. Carrots maybe. You could eat a carrot every time you want a cigarette. A carrot won't kill you and it'll help you see in the dark. I can't eat them unless they're cooked. I wish I could. I'd love to be able to eat a raw carrot. I do love the crunch you get off of it. The sound of the crunch. Do you like carrots?
TONY	I haven't had one for a while.
IMELDA	Try one now next time you want a cigarette.
TONY	Okay. *(Pause.)*
IMELDA	Are you in there on your own?
TONY	Yes.
IMELDA	Most of us are on our own. Almost all of us I'd say. Do you like being on your own?
TONY	I'm used to it.
IMELDA	I'm used to it, too. I didn't like it at first. I found it awful lonely. I have a few friends now. Do you have friends?
TONY	I've only just… I'm not long here.
IMELDA	Have you a girlfriend?
TONY	No.
IMELDA	Have you a job?
TONY	No.
IMELDA	Once you get a job, you'll get a girlfriend. You'll be right then. You're young. *(Pause.)*

IMELDA	Do you like soccer?
TONY	I used to.
IMELDA	You don't like it no more?
TONY	I don't know.
IMELDA	You can see them playing it over in the fields later and in the cages, the all-weather. They play five-a-side in the cages. Paddy watches them from here, but I can't see good enough, so I go over. They don't seem to mind. Sometimes the ball comes over the side and you'd go to get it for them, but they'd always have it got before you. They'd still say thank you, though. They're very well mannered. Sometimes they get into fights with each other. I do love a good scrap. But the other players always separate them. I like watching it on the television, too, but I prefer watching them in the cages. I prefer being outside. I don't like to be sitting down too much. I hope I never lose my legs. Please God I won't. *(Pause.)*
IMELDA	There. I can see now a bit why he does it. *(She gets to her feet.)*
IMELDA	What's your name?
TONY	Er Tony.
IMELDA	It's a pleasure to meet you, Tony.
TONY	Thanks.

(She leaves. Pause. Tony takes out his cigarettes. He has a quick look to make sure she's gone and then lights up. He looks towards the soccer in the distance. He gets up and walks a few steps away from the bench to get a better look. He stands there, smoking and watching. Lights slowly fade to black.)

Susan Millar DuMars

VIEW FROM HANNAH'S WINDOW

Hopper would paint that little white
seaside house, right now—
the sun low, the house
like the moon,
every colour, no colour, white
that's a sound; laughter,
feminine. Satisfied. Red
door and driveway gate.

He'd use this, make your eyes slide
side-to-side, red to red. Invent
a woman standing by the gate.
Apron over white dress.
Red hair lifted by the wind.
Head down; face hidden.

And though the sea is naked lips
of white and rushing blue behind,
you will not remember this.
When you close your eyes you'll see
the house that stands alone and bright;
the thin, hard arms of the red-haired woman
closing her gate for the night.

Aideen Henry

SAIBH

Saibh tends to fall in love with men she doesn't like. It is a gradual process. Some aspect repels her. With Tom, his arrogance, with John, his tendency to snort, with Wojciech, his loud aftershave. And his age. Once the man has moved from her eligible category to her definitely-not category, he is outside her radar. This is a dangerous place. She is kind and thoughtful to such men, treating them like girlfriends. Her guard is down. She is herself. Gradually she loses sight of the repelling feature and finds herself falling into them.

In time she describes a fondness for "his cute ears" or "his awful jackets", protective of the very feature that put her off in the first place. Once the in-loveness wears off however, she returns to her starting position, collecting her original dislike on her way out.

In contrast, she is wary of men she finds attractive. They could not live up to her expectations so better to carry them in her imagination and daydream about their perfection rather than discover in what way they fall short. Since Valentin was born she can't imagine falling in love with any man again.

She sits at a formica table where the finger prints and crumbs from the last occupant are still visible on its greasy surface. She is slight in frame, long-limbed and long-fingered. She finishes her coffee and examines the pastries on display, aware of her right breast slowly refilling and her left breast brimming. The bakery is in a market town, on the rail link an hour from what is now home. These towns are all alike. The bakery or café is the social hub for those with no work to go to. A young man in the corner shakes as he rolls a cigarette. A mother with two young children looks out the window into the overcast day. An unemployed older man busies himself with his newspaper, folding it carefully into quarters as he reads each section. The woman behind the counter raises her eyebrows at Saibh; her hair is trapped in a white net and her pink uniform strains across her chest.

"I'll have the cream slice, the coffee one, with a second cup of coffee, please."

"Righteo, love."

Sugar sticks to the roof of her mouth, like communion before it moistens. Puff pastry crumbles between her teeth and a blob of cream lolls on her tongue. She savours the pastry, focussing her eyes just in front of her plate. With effort she can make her eyes see darkness while still remaining open and bring her attention to the contrasting textures in her mouth. She daren't close her eyes. She licks her finger to mop up the last flaky crumbs. Mother never allowed cream cakes.

The bell over the shop door rings when she leaves the bakery. Further down the street in a charity shop, she selects a Mills & Boon from the second-hand stall. Looking through the belts and dishes, she keeps expecting to find her mother's things there. The golden hairbrush and mirror with long tarnished handles. The treasured fur coat. The trinkets collected from each foreign holiday, from a time when she still left the house. Saibh felt like someone else when she cleared that house. As though she were standing beside herself, telling herself what she should do next.

"Now, you will put all her clothes into these boxes."

The voice sounded so sure of itself. She even asked it questions.

"What about her fur coat? She really cherished that. And her jewellery and knickknacks?"

"She did. But you didn't, did you? No. So into the box with it all. You won't have to always look your best when you go out or hear anymore about how great the Clancy's daughter is doing in London now, will you? No."

The part of her packing her mother's things acquiesced. It wasn't as strong as this other self which seemed to understand the world, seemed to know her and what was best for her. Where did it come from? And where did it go to later? It knew that she shouldn't live on in her mother's house, that she didn't belong there. It knew that it was best to clear all personal things and to let the house until it was sold. It also knew that she should not be alone that night. It brought her by the hand down to the pub. It sat her down with a hot port and started her talking to Wojciech. It linked her arm to his as they walked, and led her to his bed. Wojciech was the kind of man her mother would have dissaproved of. A former olympian weight-lifter, he was a short wide man, fifteen years her senior. Oil was ingrained in the creases of his hands even after a long bath.

He stayed awake that night watching her. He was baffled to find this sylph-like creature lying next to him, her blond hair tied in a low ponytail and her slender boyish hips. He thought of his estranged wife and two sons in Poland and how in the five years he had been in Ireland he had not moved country until this night. He had found home, here in this strange child-woman, here in this bed.

The day following her mother's funeral, Saibh felt alone for the first time. She waited to conjure up that other part of herself that knew what to do, but could not reach it. She stepped in the door of her bedsit on the second floor of a Victorian house and removed her shoes. She peeled off her clothes and dropped onto her mattress on the floor for a nap. She felt a lack, a miss. She awoke from a dream in which she was kneeling inside her own transparent body, a giant hollow perspex sculpture. Piece by piece she was applying thumbnail-sized gold leaf to the inside of her body. Like a layering, a collage. She was colouring herself in.

After a bath she sat in the window seat looking out at the pink cherry blossom whose petals stuck to the droplets on the window. She could not reach anything. She felt neutered to sentience, cauterised. Though still on compassionate leave, she dressed and dropped the keys and file of her mother's house to the auctioneers and went to work. The factory was noisy and she felt relieved to gown up, put in her earplugs and start work in the sealing room. She was the only staff member who chose to work alone in that room. The others working with noisy machinery attached their earphones to iPods or to the radio. Saibh loved the silence cupped inside her earplugs. She felt it held her in, she felt minded. As though her thoughts were harnessed, concentrated and sheltered. As though her brain was hugged. Like the way a magnifying glass focuses the multidirectional rays of the sun down onto one small area. She went into a trance. Work was a dance, a rythmic movement she liked; squat to lift an empty box, gather the assembled parts and stack in the box in order of size. Press the machine down on the lid to seal. Push the box along onto the belt. Next.

At lunchtime she sat next to Cynthia. Saibh's reserve served as a contrast to Cynthia's exuberance, much as how a thin girl is often accompanied by the flattering backdrop of a fat friend. The staff were hushed until they gave her the mass card. Then Cynthia regaled the group with her most recent gossip. Saibh sat quiet, wishing she could insert her earphones again.

That Friday night she went to the cinema with Wojciech and stayed over at his apartment. Their conversations were limited by his poor English and her reluctance to speak. Their communication took the form of a kindness to each other in their exchange of words and a gentle physicality.

Weeks passed and seeing Wojciech became her new normal. She had been feeling queezy and sleeping poorly since her mother's funeral so she did not realise she was pregnant until she went to the doctor wondering if she had worms in her stomach, swollen and mobile as it was with the flickering sensation of life.

Wojciech danced her around the room with jubilant cheers in Polish at the news. He insisted she move in with him. She gave up her bedsit and moved her few things into the spare room of his ground floor apartment. He was excited enough for them both. He spent time preparing the baby's room, painting the walls and planing wood for a crib.

After baby Valentin was born, Saibh's job was reduced to a three-day week. She continued to leave the apartment at the usual time each day however and dropped Valentin off at the creche. Her trips out of town started on her free days. She felt herself led by the hand by that other part of her, accompanied to and from each town by it, but never clear on the purpose of any journey.

On the train home, Saibh removes the Mills & Boon from her bag and stares at the cover. A handsome doctor, flanked by two nurses, looks out at her; one nurse looks at him directly, the other coyly. She closes her eyes, leans her head back and lets the vibration of the train carry her for a few moments. The train stops momentarily. Out of the window she sees gold and yellow leaves flutter in the wind on a pile of stones turned black after the rainshower. The leaves look like material flowers sewn onto a child's dress. She looks down. Her breasts have doubled in size and there's a half-hour left to the journey. She stands and feels them bursting. In the toilet she pumps six ounces of milk into a container using a hand pump. She looks in the mirror, her pale face sidelit from the window. She was never close to her mother. She expected to become so once she'd had a child.

Her route walking home from the station takes her past her old bedsit. She steps inside the gates and leans her back against the copper beech hedge. This holds her weight and hides her from the street. She feels the branches prodding her through the material of her coat. Some leaves unload their cupped droplets down her neck. The lights in the bedsit are switched off. On other days she has seen a young man's shadow pass the window. She wonders does he walk around the bedsit naked as she once did, lying on the floor mattress, looking up through the tall windows at the sky and the cherry blossom branch tips that tap the window in the breeze. She looks across the garden as a blue-black raven lifts off from the bird table. On the free edge of each opening wing its feathers spread like fingers. Maybe happiness is something you only know about afterwards.

It is dark when she reaches home. Through the dining room window she sees the fire blazing. Valentin is in his high chair, sucking on his yellow duck and waving a green plastic spoon in the air. Saibh watches from the shadow, a light drizzle powdering her face. Wojciech brings the baby's dinner and sits at the table beside him. Firelight shines on Wojciech's bare shoulders and arms, an aging Hercules beside the baby. He delivers spoons full of food from a height down to Valentin's open mouth. The baby's legs kick straight and his hands slap the table so it is with difficulty that each spoonful reaches its target. Wojciech sees Saibh's face in the mirror. Through the window pane streaming with rain, her face looks transparent. Who is this woman, the mother of his son, more dilute, more distant since she moved in with him? He doesn't turn to face her. Her image retreats into the black. He hears her key turn in the lock and her call from the hall.

"I'm home."

Valentin calls out, throws his plastic spoon and arches his back out of the seat as Saibh comes into the room smiling.

Noel Duffy

DRAGONFLIES

This is dragonfly weather,
the air thick with pollen dust,
the canal bank an explosion of colour
as hedgerows come into blossom.

And then my eye catches them,
the minute flickers on the retina
of the metallic reds, greens and blues
of the dragonflies, the restless

shuttle of their flight-paths
as they dart from one point to another
plotting the water's surface
with their ghost geometries.

And then as I hunker down
at the water's edge, it is there:
the flame-red exclamation of a demoiselle
at eye level, its weightless flicker

and pulse as it hovers above
the surface, a vector of pure thought
poised and ready for movement
should I as much as quiver.

And I do quiver, stared out
there in the morning sunlight
by the glass-eyed, crystalline glare
of the living, the air trembling

with a felt absence as the dragonfly
disappears into the shadows
like a faded apparition
of what had been made

knowable to the senses.

(from *In the Library of Lost Objects* (2011) with
kind permission from Ward Wood Publishing)

Laura Ann Caffrey

THE TEACHER

The teacher paces the room
book held at eye-level,
glasses poised at the end of his nose.
He reads as he walks,
his footfall: the beat of each verse.

The classroom murmurs
to the tap of pen on desk,
but still he reads on,
he always reads on
raising the lines—a chorus
above the mob,
savouring each syllable
like a lover's name
in the hope that some day,
perhaps today,
there will be
a student who loves Bishop
almost as much as he.

Laura Ann Caffrey

AFTER THE FIGHT

I stand in my nightdress mopping
red wine from the kitchen floor,
blood after a fight.
You leave for bed, a trail of slammed
doors in your wake.

I remain downstairs unsure
of what room to go to,
a stranger in our house, and try
to figure out what to do
with the pieces of glass I've collected.
They gleam in my hand,
beautiful,
but utterly useless in their separateness.

I thought we'd built something stronger than that.

Eamonn Wall

MINE WAS A MIDWEST HOME: WILLIAM STAFFORD'S KANSAS

In her study of William Stafford's poetry, Judith Kitchen describes a "dream vision" the poet identified as one that changed his life:

> While still in high school, he biked twelve miles to camp on the banks of the Cimarron River. He spent the day, and the following night, watching as the sun fell and rose again. "No person anywhere, nothing just space, the solid earth. . . . That encounter with the size and serenity of the earth and its neighbors in the sky has never left me. The earth was my home; I would never feel lost while it held me." In Stafford's poetry there is often an attempt to duplicate, at least in feeling, that original dream vision. Often, when this happens, the "earth" becomes the "world," and a distinction is made between the *place* of living and a larger, natural order which governs all life. (15)

My purpose will be to explore and test the depth and complexity of Stafford's dream vision to show how it is manifested in his aesthetic and poetics, to identify the forms and shapes these beliefs and theories take in some key poems from his first two collections, *West of Your City* (1960) and *Traveling Through the Dark* (1962), and to point out the function that place, both the Midwest and West, plays in these volumes.

Stafford was born in Hutchinson, Kansas, in 1914 and died in Portland, Oregon, in 1993. When an adolescent during the Depression, his family moved to various towns in Kansas as his father sought whatever work was available, and Stafford helped out by working at various odd jobs, at one time providing the family with its only source of income (Kitchen 3). Though his family did not belong to one particular church, they attended various places of worship, and Stafford learned from his parents "the value of hard moral decisions and the security of firmly held convictions" (Kitchen 3). He enrolled at the University of Kansas, working his through college by waiting on tables, and began to write (Kitchen 4). At the outbreak of World War II,

Stafford registered as a pacifist and "spent the duration of the war in camps and projects for conscientious objectors in Arkansas, California and Illinois, working on soil conservation projects, forestry, and fighting fires" (Kitchen 4). His experience as an objector to a popular war and a worker in various C. O. camps was as important to his moral and political outlook as his "dream vision" on the banks of the Cimarron was to his poetical and ecological views, though Stafford would surely have believed that the two events could not have been separated. His first book was the memoir *Down in My Heart* (1947) in which he chronicled his time served in the camps. "The Mob Scene at McNeil" is one of the most memorable chapters from this work, capturing the hostility that pacifists of that era could face from bemused fellow Americans:

> When we had hiked into McNeil we had found a few men loafing around in the shade. The stores were closed; Main Street extended a block each way from the depot and then relaxed into a sand road that wandered among scattered houses. We too relaxed for our Sunday afternoon. Bob set up his drawing board; George got out his tablet and pen; and I sat leaning against a telephone pole and began to read—among dangerous men. (Every War Has Two Losers 16)

The three had come quietly to town from their camp in Magnolia, Arkansas, to write and paint, when they were accosted by a small group of local men. When word got around of their presence in McNeil, the crowd grew larger and angrier. Stafford and his companions were accused of being German spies and there was some talk of a lynching. Eventually, the trio was rescued by the police, who escorted them back to their camp. Stafford has said that he learned his pacifism from his mother and that his time in the C. O. camps "was four years of reinforcement of my mother's point of view" (*Every War Has Two Losers* 144); that "the underground, peacetime underground, is essential for the health, not of the state, but of the people" (*Every War Has Two Losers* 27); and concluded a poem entitled "In Camp" with the couplet, "In camps like that, if I should go again, / I'd still study the gospel and play the accordion" (*The Darkness Around Us Is Deep* 121).

*

"Our Home" and "Ceremony" are two significant poems that appear in "Midwest", *West of Your City*'s first section. The volume's sections follow Stafford's own progression—from the childhood world of rural Kansas of the opening section to the "Far West" of section two, indicating his residence in California after the War, to the more abstract "Outside" of the third section which suggests that he had claimed another place formed from a synthesis of "Midwest" and "Far West". However, Stafford's idea of time is not always linear and topographical demarcations are frequently artificial. If one believes, as I do, that the West begins when one crosses the Missouri River and that Kansas is more Western than Midwestern, then one might say that Stafford was a Westerner from birth. Frequently throughout his poetry, for all his years of living in the Far West, as he calls it, Stafford's imagination, unfettered by linear time, circles back to Kansas from whose landscapes he first absorbed language. Today, he is claimed by both the Midwest and West. Book-ended by its opening and closing lines, "Our Home" combines full-hearted celebration of place and hard irony. The opening lines, "Mine was a midwest home—you can keep your world," reminds us that Kansas is both remote and a world onto itself (29). Its locals are proud of what they have and the poem's opening promises to bring the reader in on the secret. Immediately, we are deflated by the "plain black hats" and "our code" of line two and the imperative of the third indicating that the locals think that Kansas is closer to heaven that any other place in the US, or on earth for that matter (29). The light is "wan" and "the sun. . . over our town" was "like a blade" (30). The assertive ending "Wherever we looked the land would hold us up" brings us back to Stafford's "dream vision," cited at the outset, from which he had learned that "the earth was [his] home; I would never feel lost while it held me" (30).

While the opening of "Our Home" asserts individuality the closing testifies to the land, the force that will sustain us. Of course, "the land" can be read broadly or narrowly–as the world, or as Kansas. Geographically, it might be seen to represent interiors—hearts, souls, imaginations. Reviewing *West of Your City* in 1961, James Dickey noted that Stafford's "natural mode of speech is a gentle, mystical, half-mocking and highly personal day dreaming about the landscape of the western United States. . . . Let Mr. Stafford keep pouring it out. It is all good, all to his purpose" (3-4).

Water, another element underlining Stafford's connection to the land, is to be found in "Ceremony," a poem recounting an incident in which a man is bitten by a muskrat. Kitchen summarizes the poem's basic elements: "the poem roots him in his native Kansas plains but foreshadows his embracing all the land. Here, the river—fluid, deep, endless—is established as one of Stafford's natural images. In poem after poem, rivers, their currents and hidden depths, become symbols for movement and mystery. They are places he will look for meaning" (30). Like Joyce's Liffey, Stafford's Ninnescah is the circular, living repository of place and knowledge, and of immense physical, symbolic and moral importance. The blood that enters the river, and which will flow into the ocean, is encoded with the man's history, and with all of the histories of ancestors from whose parts he has been created: it will be renewed and altered by its journey and by what it will have absorbed from saltwater, before being absorbed into cloud and returned to land. As in marriage, the bodies of muskrat and man are entwined to inherit a new, common history and acknowledge a shared fate. Above it all, an owl hails achieved wisdom and loudly echoes the depth of this exciting, physical intercourse:

> While in the woods an owl started quavering
> with drops like tears I raised my arm.
> Under the bank a muskrat was trembling
> with meaning my hand would wear forever. (*Stories That Could Be True* 30)

In one of his greatest poems, "At the Bomb Testing Site," Stafford negates the anthropological primacy of the human being by placing the lizard at the center of the poem, as the living creature best able to understand, absorb, and register the magnitude of what is being unleashed by the explosion of an atomic device. The lizard is more ancient than the human, more attuned to the earth, and it possesses the spread of history more profoundly that we do. We humans may have our intelligence, but what have we made of it, Stafford wonders rhetorically. Here is the poem in full:

> At noon in the desert a panting lizard
> waited for history, its elbows tense,
> watching the curve of a particular road
> as if something might happen.

It was looking at something farther off
than people could see, an important scene
acted in stone for little selves
at the flute end of consequences.

There was just a continent without much on it
under a sky that never cared less.
Ready for a change, the elbows waited.
The hands gripped hard on the desert. (*Stories That Could Be True* 41)

In his praise of this majestic poem, Charles Simic writes that "true form is the product of an extraordinary vision" and that "in the meantime, we can say with Heidegger that poems such as this one open the largest view of the earth, sky, mortals and their true and false gods" (219-20).

When it was put to him in his *Paris Review* interview that the great sense of space evident in his work was the result of his growing up in Kansas, Stafford's reply was characteristically mild, "I sometimes have thought about that, yes. In our world at least half the world was sky; that is the way I've sometimes phrased it to myself. I mean there's the land, but it isn't as big as the sky" (27). Richard Hugo is more definite when he writes that "Stafford's original external landscape, and (since he is an honest poet) his internal one as well, is Kansas. Flat vistas, a harsh cruel weather but one that comes from far off, can be predicted, even spotted early, and consequently prepared for (strategy): drab customs, at least in Stafford's day, drab towns, repressive social codes. This is the Kansas represented in the poems" (117). Hugo perfectly describes the ironies and ambiguous language, as well as the open spaces, present in the *West of Your City*, and he goes on to argue that, at first, Stafford found it difficult to adapt to the landscape of the Pacific Northwest because "hills and mountains are in your way [and] the deep, long, uninterrupted gaze is rarely possible" (117). It is a less defined and rigid world though one, Hugo maintains, that Stafford was eventually able to adapt his poetic vision to. Of course, Stafford's literary imagination and moral outlook was formed by family, politics, and education. However, his "dream vision," which made so much possible for him, was a gift from nature. The tonal register of Midwestern poetry is often quite flat, as it is in Stafford's work too, and an indication of the extent to which landscape and sky have influenced language. Whereas Stafford's themes are large ones, his language is muted and avoids ornament. The music is subtle but true, the work driven, as with Whitman, by voice. His free verse forms, though engaged with the American tradition, derive their shapes from the land and sky of his native Kansas.

The title poem of Stafford's second collection *Traveling Through the Dark* has been widely anthologized and is undoubtedly his most-read poem. Whereas *West of Your City* was published by a small press in California, this volume found a New York publisher, received a National Book Award, and brought Stafford to the forefront of the American poetry scene where he remained for the rest of his life. It was the first of many awards he would receive. The incident related in the poem is simply stated: a driver, seeing a dead deer by the roadside, pulls over out of curiosity, empathy, or from a desire to be a witness. He discovers that the deer is pregnant and, for the moment, the fawn is alive inside of her dead body:

> My fingers touching her side brought me the reason—
> her side was warm; her fawn lay there waiting,
> alive, still, never to be born. (61)

The poem is full of the personifications, contrasts, and balancing of elements, which Jonathan Holden sees as Stafford's formalist inheritance, such as the parallel drawn between the living fawn inside the deer's body and the engine purring inside the body of the car:

> The car aimed ahead its lowered parking lights;
> under the hood purred the steady engine.
> I stood in the glare of the warm exhaust turning red;
> around our group I could hear the wilderness listen. (61)

All of his critics have addressed and analyzed this poem to indicate how central it is to Stafford's work and to show how well it brings into sharp focus many themes that underline it. Present here, in various forms, are the three central themes of Stafford's work as identified by Judith Kitchen: "family and love; the West and wilderness and communion with nature; and technology with the notion that the nation will fail to put it to proper use" (10). The symbolic thread running through the poem is also rich: the man in the poem representing all men; the deer standing for all animals and all mothers, these thoughtful mergings being aspects of the slippage that Stafford favors, and which make it possible for him to see everyone and everything in the world as not just connected but one; and the darkness providing entry into a deeper space where the surfaces of form and identity can be stripped away. For Stafford, "meaningful events take place in isolation and silence" and here the precise location is the edge of a road (Kitchen 15). Both this poem and "At the Bomb Testing Site" "demonstrate the encroachment of mechanized society on the wilderness" and prepare the reader for a hard re-examination of history, and the tough choices that must be made to secure a future (Kitchen 41). Both mark Stafford as an eco-poet, among other things.

> On an aesthetic level, what makes the poem so effective and beautiful is the use of sound. Because the system is not regular—neither in metrics nor rhyme—no one element stands out though all—syntax, diction, alliteration, personification and assonance—float seamlessly together to build a voice and tone. As Simic points out in relation to "At the Bomb Testing Site," "true form is the product of an extraordinary vision," and this is equally true here, and in all of Stafford's greatest poems (219). Stafford has said that "sound comes out of the language right while you're living the language," indicating that for him it is heard rather than invented (Kitchen 109). Of syllabics he notes:

> I like how syllables do-si-do along. I am not after rhyme—so limited, so mechanical. No I want all the syllables to be there like a school of fish, flashing, relating to other syllables in other words (even words not in this poem of course), fluently carrying the reader by subliminal felicities all the way to the limber last line. (Kitchen 107)

One reason why "Traveling Through the Dark" has been so honored is because it so successfully succeeds on these complex registers of sound. Henry Taylor sees in Stafford's work "a delicate scheme" where the meter is "unstable. . . yet the rhythmical rightness of each line is firmly there, not to be quarreled with" (221). William Heyen finds in Stafford's poetics that "full rhymes are infrequent, pyrotechnics are at a minimum, but the lines are held together by a sort of unstudied point-counterpoint" and finds, quoting John Crowe Ransom, that in Stafford's work "sound patterns give us the feeling of ritual" (123-24). Stafford's thematic technique of aligning objects with ideas (home and self, for example) is replicated in his use of words and how they sound:

But in an essay, "Finding the Language," Stafford describes his own faith in "certain reinforcing patterns of sound which the language, as if by chance, has taken up into itself. That is, all syllables tend to slide by inherent quality toward certain meanings, either because of varying demands on the throat in utterance, or because of relations among clusters of syllables which have become loaded with associated meanings, and so on." (Heyen 123)

In his reading of Stafford, Richard Howard links these sound patterns to similar patterns found in Old English poetry (104). A final element or linkage can be deduced from what Stafford noted in his *Prairie Schooner* interview:

We already have the skills for poetry when we learn to talk. What we need is the faith to carry right through with it. Besides the language, and all the opportunities in it—the language we all know so well—there is also that other dimension, those patterns that may lead if we can follow right. I might put it in William Blake's lines that go something like; "I give you the end of a golden string, just roll it into a ball and it will lead you into the gate built in Jerusalem's wall. . . ." (Heyen 130)

The language of Stafford's poetry is both literary and demotic, and of the present and of both the near and distant pasts. By listening carefully, recording and ordering, Stafford seeks wider linkages (across time and space) between the written and the oral. In terms of diction and sound, as Richard Howard and others have testified, Stafford's poetry owes much to, and is rooted in, a literary tradition that goes back to Old English poems. In this respect, his work is similar to John Berryman's; whereas *The Dream Songs* are modern in shape, in syntax and diction they are traditional, Elizabethan in Berryman's case. At the same time, Stafford's verse is guided by and most tenderly formed by Kansas space and American English. Both his line and stanza have been shaped, first, by landscape and, second, by modernism.

In many respects, the world as he understood it, growing up in Kansas, is our world and the choices he made are the choices we too must make. As time has moved on, so has Stafford's vision. His work has not stuck in his time; rather, it has moved on to embrace and explain ours. In outlook and form, William Stafford's work displays a remarkable unity, and it gives the impression, as Judith Kitchen reminds us, of being "written all at once. . .from a central unchanging sensibility" though one that remained current and active as it accepted "flux as part of its natural method" (9). Evidence of this can be found in *The Darkness Around Us Is Deep: Selected Poems of William Stafford*, Robert Bly's selection, in which the poems are grouped thematically: we will not notice the forsaking of chronology so seamlessly does the volume read. Stafford's work habits were also consistent, almost to a fault. Rising early, at 3 or 4 a.m., to have a quiet space before his family stirred and before the necessity of leaving home for work, and placing himself on his couch, he wrote "perhaps, a poem a day for over forty years and published over sixty books during his lifetime," even though he had passed beyond his mid-forties by the time his first collection had appeared (Kitchen 2). Many critics have argued that he wrote too much and published too many weak poems, and this argument has validity. In my view, Stafford's greatest work is to be found in *West of Your City* and *Traveling Through the Dark*, his first two volumes, and in his third, *The Rescued Year* (1966), which consists of new poems, work from *West of Your City* and from his University of Iowa dissertation. As a poet, writing theorist, political philosopher and environmentalist, Stafford's is a voice that continues to be heard and needs to be attended to.

WORKS CITED

Dickey, James. "William Stafford". Tom Andrews ed. *On William Stafford: The Worth of Local Things*. Ann Arbor: The University of Michigan Press, 1993, 3-4.

Heyen, William. "William Stafford's Allegiances". Tom Andrews ed. *On William Stafford: The Worth of Local Things*. Ann Arbor: The University of Michigan Press, 1993, 121-131.

Holden, Jonathan. *The Mark to Turn: A Reading of William Stafford's Poetry*. Lawrence: University of Kansas Press, 1976.

Howard, Richard. "'Tell Us What You Deserve,' the Whole World Said." Tom Andrews ed. *On William Stafford: The Worth of Local Things*. Ann Arbor: The University of Michigan Press, 1993, 104-112.

Kitchen, Judith. *Writing the World: Understanding William Stafford*. Corvallis: Oregon State University Press, 1999.

Simic, Charles. "'At the Bomb Testing Site.'" Tom Andrews ed. *On William Stafford: The Worth of Local Things*. Ann Arbor: The University of Michigan Press, 1993, 219-220.

Stafford, William. *The Darkness Around Us Is Deep: Selected Poems of William Stafford*. Robert Bly ed. New York: HarperPerennial, 1993.

. . . *Every War Has Two Losers: William Stafford on Peace and War.* Kim Stafford ed. Minneapolis: Milkweed Editions, 2003.

. . . "The Mob Scene at McNeil." *Every War Has Two Losers: William Stafford on Peace and War.* Kim Stafford ed. Minneapolis: Milkweed Editions, 2003, 13-23.

. . . "The Art of Poetry: The *Paris Review* Interview with William Young." *The Answers Are Inside the Mountains: Meditations on the Writing Life.* Paul Merchant and Vincent Wixon eds. Ann Arbor: University of Michigan Press, 2003, 22-41.

. . . *Stories That Could Be True: New and Collected Poems.* New York: Harper & Row, 1977.

Taylor, Henry. "'Thinking for Berky': Millions of Intricate Moves." Tom Andrews ed. On William Stafford: The Worth of Local Things. Ann Arbor: The University of Michigan Press, 1993, 221

Moya Cannon

FINGER-FLUTING IN MOON-MILK

We are told that usually, not always,
a woman's index finger
is longer than her ring-finger,
that, in men, it is usually the opposite,
that the moon-milk in this cave
retains the finger prints and flutings
of over forty children, women and men
who lived in the late Palaeolithic.

Here, in the river-polished Dordogne,
as the last ice-sheets started to retreat
northwards from the Pyrenees,
in a cave which is painted with gentle-faced
horses and long files of mammoths,
a woman, it seems, with a baby on her hip
trailed her fingers down through
the soft, white substance
extruded by limestone cave-walls
and the child copied her.

Today, the finger flutings remain clear,
the moon-milk remains soft.
As we trundle through the cave's maze
in our open-topped toy train
we are forbidden to touch it.

With no gauge to measure sensibility
we cannot know what portion
of our humanity we share
with someone who showed a child
how to sign itself in moon-milk
one day, late in the Old Stone Age.

Rouffignac, 2010

Moya Cannon

CLASSIC HAIR DESIGNS

Every day they are dropped off
at *Classic Hair Designs*,
sometimes in taxis,
sometimes by daughters,
often by middle-aged sons
in sober coats
who pull in tight by the kerb
and stride around to the door
and offer an arm.

How important this last,
or almost last, vestige
of our animal pelt is.
How we cherish it –
the Egyptians' braided bob,
those banded Grecian curls,
the elaborate patterns of Africa,
the powdered, teetering pompadour,
the sixties' long shining fall over a guitar,

and the fine halo
of my almost-blind,
ninety-two year old neighbour,
permed and set
in the style
in which she stepped out
with her young man
after the second world war.

James Harpur

A CLERIHEW FOR ADRIAN FRAZIER

Professor Adrian Frazier
Is sharp as a razier;
More Quiet Man than John Ford,
Much hairier than Gonne (Maud).

James Harpur

CARPE DIEM
After Horace Ode 1.11

For Adrian Frazier

We cannot tell what fate has planned for us
So don't inquire or bother reading tea leaves.
God knows, we could enjoy a few more winters
Or maybe this one, smashing ocean waves
Against the rocks, will be our last. Who's to say?
Be smart, relax, enjoy a good French wine
And trim your hopes to match a life that's brief.
Even as I type these words begrudging time
Is slipping by. So, come on, *seize the day*:
Trusting the future is a recipe for grief.

Deirdre Sullivan

SEEING RED

Outside in the forest, there is deep snow. It brightens the earth and makes this place shine with a false cleanliness that I can hardly stand. I turn my face from the window and concentrate on feeling almost nothing. It has been a pale and honest morning, spent cleaning things and rearranging cushions, distracting myself with pretty, useless, touches. Embroidered stars. Some holly in a vase. The wooden floors are cold and getting colder. I do not want to light the fire yet. I do not want to waste the golden wood. It saddens me to think of it so old and strong that turns to ash so easily. We all will I suppose. My feet are numb and so I pile the smallest twigs and twists of yellowed paper on the grate.

When I was a small girl something happened to me in the forest. I can't recall exactly what it was. It's hard to trust tales from the lips of grandmothers; they come out wrong, too dirty or too clean. Since then I have not the same about the forest: I liked it once I think or think I think. It's beautiful but on its inky edges something stirs to fidget with my gut. It's getting dark, my husband will be home soon. I bite down on my lips to make them red.

The bread I made today is warm and soft. It permeates the rooms: a smell to welcome him when he comes back. I must have learnt the recipe by instinct, when first I tried my loaves were nigh inedible: a source of shame and not a source of comfort. But now I find that I enjoy preparing food, for all the act of eating saddens me. It feels so wasteful, something for myself and no-one else to do, for if I eat it's usually alone. I wish sometimes to be a broad-hipped matron, unassailable and somehow pure. The in-between is what scares me, curvy and delicious. Ripening. Could I protect my bones' delicious marrow then? I can't protect it now; I'm porcelain and hollow, like a bird, or like a china bird with onyx bright eyes. To have always just alighted on mantelpieces but never flown anywhere, for fear of crumbling. I blink and I prepare a charming house to match my charming figure. 'How can someone so small know so much?' he says 'so many woman's things'. He spends inordinate amounts of the evenings studying my face. What he feels there must content him, he lets go and I release my breath. I wonder what he knows of me, his gaze deciphers codes that may exist alien entirely to me. Barrel-chested hieroglyphs and phrenologic signs that men of his ilk know. The crackle of the fire I will set. Its glow upon the soft rope of my hair. He likes to brush it with his left hand's fingers. The other rests in warning on my neck. I light the flame. The tapers and the oil lamps. I know that I am wasteful but I need the light so I can tell it's him and not a stranger who will turn the latch and greet me with his voice. The sky pelt dark. The sky is filled with little glinting teeth.

When I was a small girl I rested my head on my grandmothers lap in the lull of the evenings. I closed my eyes and listened to her speak. Her lap was soft and stale, she smelt of sweat and pine, mixed with the musk peculiar to old women. Sometimes I think I smell it on myself. Her tales were strange, of twice-born fiends and women made of knives, of wild unfettered things who sup on people, who start at toes and finish up with eyes. I did not think them strange, not at the time, enamoured as I was with the attention, her busy hands removing tangles, lice, and plaiting and unplaiting. The voice that wove. And I was so afraid and so delighted. I wanted more, I wanted her to stop.

The window panes are clear but edged with frost. There are no curtains. It is winter but the trees still wear their leaves. They are lovely to observe, especially when the sun is at its lowest but underneath their clothes they grip skeletal, poke and drag at fabric and at skin. It is not easy to be lost in a forest, plump and soft when everything is harsh and grasping out. A forest is lovely to look at but only to look at. Once inside you can't look anymore, everything is muted and in shadow. Supplicants are what the forest likes. The clearest of directions are of no use and once inside this soon becomes apparent. To find your way, you must give in, must root like a pig until the paths unravel, nosing here and there, increasingly perturbed. Desperate, submitting to the tangling and the staining. The only way you learn. Shallow breaths come quick and mist the glass. My fingers touch the cold and trace a pattern. A leaf, two leaves suspended without branches. I use my sleeve to wipe those leaves away.

The dark is rough outside and something cries in panic or in fear. It's far away and I try not to listen. The snow is clean and weighs upon the murk. Purity that burns through films and fells and, in departure, shows things as they are. It is not a good idea to notice things too much here. Slitted eyes that lead to slitted bellies. Things with plans meander through the woods. Pretty children hide their faces through the paths, they daub themselves with moss. Conceal the smell of soft bread and cheap wine. The gifts they bring. They hide the gifts like shame. I've never even thought I was with child. My ribs jut out too hungrily, like spikes, they'd not know how to nourish something small and soft and pulsing. He would like a child. Not for itself but for what it would mean. What villagers would say. What a man he is, so strong and potent, that he could make a china doll his vessel. Fill her to the brim with little mewling versions of himself. Small, hungry fisted men, raging and biting gummily would be just what he'd want. Not one like me. I'd hate to have a daughter, would scrape her out to red blood upon snow. I rarely bleed, but I would bleed for her sake, and never mind, and never count the drops. And I would wait and chase away the crows. A boy would be too strong to kill. All snout and hunger, he would suckle all my sadness out, and leave me husklike, motioning weakly, made of ash and breath. My husband's meaty heart would break in two, if ever he suspected. Can muscles break, an angry messy breaking? Gobbled up. I would be gobbled up.

I know what I must do to keep safe. Stay on the path, one thing after another. I fill my man a basket full of foods. Swaddle them in tea-towels and brown paper. Bread and ale and cheese and meat and apples. Things that can be eaten in big bites. What a big lunch he eats, this husband of mine, with his axe on his shoulder he strides the way he munches, into the forest wide and unafraid. And now that's done. He's not yet home but everything is in readiness. He's not yet home but everything is tidy, neat and properly arranged. My mind drifts but my industry never wavers. I don't know what would happen if it did. The fire blazes weakly, nuzzling the grate with half an ashy heart. Still, it will suffice, when he returns cold and hungry. The necessary comforts will await him: dinner, fire, and by it his so good and pretty wife slowly carding brittle wool. These are things my husband likes to see. His proverbs drip with idle hands and rods. He instructs and sometimes he is sad to see my hands so chapped and raw from all my household labours that he clucks his tongue, and rubs them soft with butter. He has a rare kindness in him, something seldom seen. I wonder if he's happy. Sky pools darkest blue and night stalks day. Soon I'll hear his hobnails, louder and louder, on the path. Soon, but not so soon as to deter me. There is time yet. Not a surfeit, but still; there is time.

When I was a small girl my granny made me things. Things to eat and sometimes things to wear. I am not a small girl any more, my clever fingers sew and spin and weave. My hands are practised now, they assemble such delicious things. Savouries and sweets. My voice I keep so soothing and so soft. My body lithe and hairless where there ought to be no hair. Still. When I was a small girl something happened to me in the forest. Good things too had happened before that but this was something altogether strange and best forgotten. It might have not been what I think it was. Sometimes I would like to be a child again, and other times a woman made of snow.

In a place hollowed beneath the floorboards something lurks. Hidden deep but I have found it out. His skillful sausage fingers built this house and kept it, big and ready but I have cleaned it every single day since his child bride was rescued and brought home I am privy to its secrets now, can sense its nooks and crannies more than he. I shake the dread thing he has hidden out. Oh, but it is lovely, soft and rough and altogether shameless. It almost smells of skin and bloodied breath. Warmer already, I unlace my shift. Piece by piece I thoroughly disrobe, and hold my treasure up and spread it wide. It soon is wrapped around my face and body. Thus enlaced I close my eyes and listen for a footstep on the gravel. The edges of my mind are softening. Something is melting. Something is falling down. My heart beat slows, womb snug and belly safe. I ache for things I know and do not know. Something here is straining, soon it will break and I will feel it break and still do nothing. My face is covered with the safest caul. Membrane meeting membrane, I allow myself to wish for things unspoken. Foreign things that glint beneath the snow and could be filth but maybe are not filth. Unremembered colours, rancid tongues that slaver but wash clean. Well-met dangers, safety of a little worried maiden, hurry, hurry. Hoods are funny things. Mostly dark, evoking executioners. Eyelids flicker. Wet salt upon fur.

Thomas Dillon Redshaw

THREE PLACES IN NEW ENGLAND

1950

Under the clean August heat a child naps
in a dim room on whose yellow wallpaper
float white China temples consecrated
to stylized mercy.
                          Waxy, stiff, the paper
shades let in the light of the East, waning
that afternoon. This side of the house rests
now in near shade. Someone has raised
both sashes from the sill so the shades
waver in freshening salt drafts. Tap,
tap of the green crocheted shade-pulls,
each a threaded circle.
                          Resting light, turn,
turn to glimpse between sill and sash
that latitude of arresting blue—that
unparalleled dream of clear sailing.

Thomas Dillon Redshaw

Empty Beach

The yellow bus had stopped on the north shoulder
of the coast road where it curved inland & west.
Black block letters under empty windows
bore the forgotten Puritan names of suburban
townships. From those doors the driver had left
Folded open,
              I could see the path across then
down the berm, under the feathery leafage
of the sumac wood, to the heaped stones, then
shelly sand of the wide & empty beach stretching
flat away, then darkening in neap tide, glistening
just at a far-off horizon.
                That one sight, then.
Was why I had been brought in my sleep here
And left to stare bare-headed like someone's child.

Thomas Dillon Redshaw

A Cup by Kit Cornell

I did not buy the real thing at the market
on hospital hill that morning, but
took away the perfect postcard of it—
a bookmark, a memento—as if the glaze
gave a scene we will travel into but not
return from
              —a gray & sandy foreshore,
darker where the tide laps back—
                          and where
we will remain gazing at the blue gleam
lightly turning across darker waters to
the lip of the cup lit up like a line
of low cloud lying easterly on a horizon.

Out there, the cup waits empty & ever
ready to fill, raise, and pass hand-to-hand.

Thomas Kilroy

Extract from BLAKE

SCENE SIX
A dark cell in the Asylum.

A pool of light on a darkened stage. Blake and Catherine sit close together on a simple bench in this light. The outline of figures, asylum keepers, in the dark background. At some height, as if suspended in the air, the lit head and shoulders of Dr. Hibbel, Superintendent of Finchley Grange Lunatic Asylum, observing Blake and his wife Catherine in the cell and recording details in his notebook.

BLAKE: Why are we here? There is something afoot but I don't know what! And what else did he say to you, our little doctor of madhouses?

CATHERINE: He said I'd be locked up, too, for the rest of my life if I didn't come to my senses. Is it so easy to become a mad woman?

BLAKE: Did he indeed? He would be a tyrant, our puny doctor, but that he does not have the stomach for it.

CATHERINE: Men in charge of buildings can be such fools. It must be the buildings that make them so. Do you know, William, I've been keeping my eyes peeled about this place. There is no way out. Once you open one door there is another locked before you. And another. And another. Where is the open door and blessed daylight?

BLAKE: But my release? He spoke of my release, you say?

CATHERINE:	I just want us to go home, William –
BLAKE:	Conditions? He attached conditions to my – release?
CATHERINE:	Listen, William. I've been thinking –
BLAKE:	It makes me fearful, Kate, when you start your thinking –
CATHERINE:	Oh, it does does it! You believe I'm a noodle, is that it? Such nerve!
BLAKE:	Why have they left us like this? Where are the others? I do not like it. It is a net to catch us but how I cannot understand.
CATHERINE:	We could make love, William. Now. Before they return and take us to those cells. I want you inside me so much. Then I'd feel they could never harm us no matter what they might do afterwards!
BLAKE:	We are being watched!
CATHERINE:	*(Jump)* Watched? Who is watching?
BLAKE:	I do not know. I simply know we are watched and I do not speak of the great Eye of God above our heads.
CATHERINE:	Hold my hand, William, please! Be close to me!
BLAKE:	You are not answering my question, Kate. This doctor with his keys and bolts. What does he want? What are his conditions?
CATHERINE:	He says you're mad, William –
BLAKE:	Why, then, he's in good company! Half of London proclaims my madness. Am I as mad as the king? That is the question? Am I as mad as the old men who send our youth to die in

red uniforms so that Commerce and Religion may join hands in profit? Am I as mad as those who would ensnare a child in a mill or a black woman in Surinam? These are the questions they should answer.

CATHERINE: You are no more mad than I am and that's proof of the pudding. But for some reason – why I don't know – the little doctor must have you mad.

BLAKE: If they would but let us work, Kate, why then this place is as good as another. In some ways better, I do think. We do not have to go to the shop and there are none of the usual idiots to distract us on street corners. All I need is my graver and copper plates and –

CATHERINE: *(Loudly)* All you need is to pretend! Pretend! For but a little while!

BLAKE: Pretend! What is this babbling?

CATHERINE: *(Rush)* The doctor says if you confess to madness you can be cured. All you need do is pretend madness then pretend cure and we may go home again, William. Home! *(Pause)* See! He wouldn't know either way, the doctor.

BLAKE: What did you say? Just now. Pretend – pretend –

CATHERINE: Tell the foolish little man what he wants to hear! That you're mad when compelled by your visions! Then he will think he sees into your mind and how it works, poor, poor fool that he is. He will tot up his ledger and move your name from the mad list to the sane list. He will sign his name to the paper and we will go home!

BLAKE: And pretend? And lie!

CATHERINE: In a place like this there's no lie. No truth −

BLAKE: *(Beating his breast)* Lies and truth are in here! Here!
               Not in places.

CATHERINE: Oh, but you are so self-righteous!

BLAKE: *(He cannot listen)* Silence!

CATHERINE: You're so puffed up with your righteousness, Mr. Blake,
               that you can't see what's in front of you. Head in the heavens
               and tripping over stones, you are.

BLAKE: How dare you speak thus!

CATHERINE: I talk out of love for you, though you
               won't hear it!

BLAKE: Love! Love!

CATHERINE: You remember, William? In Lambeth? When we sat
               in the garden without a stitch on and agreed, you and I,
               that that's all that matters in the end? Love −

BLAKE: I have traced the picture of all that lives and all that is beyond
               life −

CATHERINE: I know, William −

BLAKE: Nor are these visions my own, no, I am but the secretary and
               the author dictates to me from Eternity −

CATHERINE: All this I know, William −

BLAKE:	This very morning by the grilled window within there I heard again, as often before, the lark's song, his little throat labouring with inspiration, every feather vibrating with Divine Breath. I heard again, too, the silence of Nature as it listened to the bird and the awful Sun paused once more on the mountain top unwilling to move until the bird had finished his divine song of praise.
CATHERINE:	But you don't need to say all this to me, Will! I know!
BLAKE:	All of this you would have me deny, Catherine Boucher.
CATHERINE:	I'm Catherine Blake and I don't deny you!
BLAKE:	No longer by my side – my wife!
CATHERINE:	Don't reject me, William! Don't! I beg of you.
BLAKE:	You've gone over to the other side –
CATHERINE:	Why do you put me away like this? Why?
BLAKE:	Because you do not do not follow me without question.
CATHERINE:	I see. There's nothing so bad as the pride of the man who says he sees God. You put me aside like this once before. Remember? When we were unable to conceive a child.
BLAKE:	*(Hands to ears)* Stop it! Stopstopstop!
CATHERINE:	As always I took the blame. I was trying to protect you from yourself. What a fool I was. Yes, I said, yes, I can't conceive. But you know and I know, William, that this was not true. The truth was that you were unable to give me a child.

111

BLAKE:	I will not listen to you! I'm not listening, woman!

CATHERINE:	You must listen! You are but a man like other men, William Blake, at the end of the day. No better, no worse when you stand naked before your Maker. You talk of facing the demon. The demon is not in others. It is in ourselves! Look to yourself, William Blake!

BLAKE:	*(Threatening to hit her)* Get out of my sight, you, you – before I –

Dr. Hibbel:	*(Claps his hands)* Remove the woman! I have heard enough

He disappears from view. Female keepers come forward and take Catherine off into the darkness.

CATHERINE:	*(Scream)* William!

A loud, thumping noise. Blake puts his hands to his head.

BLAKE:	*(Very distressed)* Children? I don't need children! I have my own children. They come from my head in a line, down through the ages and their children and their children's children will follow to the ultimate degree. "And these are my Sons, the Sons of Los and Enitharmon. Rintrah and Palambron Theotormon Bromion Reuben Judah David Luther Milton These are the daughters off my visions, Oothoon Leutha Moab Rahab Tirzah Mary"—"And myriads more Sons and daughters to whom our love increased To each according to the multiplication of the multitudes—"
	(Breaking down) I do not need children.

Lights down

John Montague

A CHRISTMAS CARD

Christmas in Brooklyn,
the old El flashes by.
A man plods along pulling
his three sons on a sleigh;
soon his whole family
will vanish away.

My long lost father
trudging home through
this strange, cold city,
its whirling snows,
unemployed and angry,
living off charity.

Finding a home only
in brother John's speakeasy.
Beneath the stoop
a flare of revelry.
And yet you found time
to croon to your last son.

Dear Father, a grace note.
That Christmas you did
find a job, guarding
a hole in the Navy Yard.
Elated, you celebrated
so well you fell in.

Not a model father.
'I was only happy
when I was drunk,'
building a fire in
a room I was working in.

Still, you soldiered on
all those years alone in
a Brooklyn boarding house
without your family
until the job was done;
and then limped home.

John Montague

THE WATER CARRIER

Twice daily I carried water from the spring,
Morning before leaving for school, and evening;
Balanced as a fulcrum between two buckets.

A bramble-rough path ran to the river
Where you stepped carefully across slime-topped stones,
With corners abraded as bleakly white as bones.

At the widening pool (for washing and cattle)
Minute fish flickered as you dipped,
Circling to fill, with rust-tinged water.

The second or enamel bucket was for spring water
Which after racing through a rushy meadow,
Came bubbling in a broken drain-pipe,

Corroded wafer-thin with rust.
It ran so pure and cold it fell
Like manacles of ice upon the wrists.

You stood until the bucket brimmed,
Inhaling the musty smell of unpicked berries,
That heavy greenness fostered by water.

Recovering the scene, I had hoped to stylize it,
Like the portrait of an Egyptian water carrier;
But halt, entranced by slight but memoried life.

I sometimes come to take the water there,
Not as a return or refuge, but some pure thing,
Some living source, half-imagined and half-real,

Pulses in the fictive water that I feel.

Patricia Byrne

AMERICA TO GALWAY

Boston's Washington Street seems to go on forever. Mostly built in the early-nineteenth century it is Boston's longest street that extends south-westward from the city in long straight lines through the suburb of Dedham. It is the route of the 34A bus that purrs its way past *Jimmy's Pizzeria* and the *Creative Kids Academy* into the sleepy town of East Walpole, where I alight to the harsh-sweet smell of hot asphalt.

When I left Boston—some thirteen miles away—the city air was heavy with a murky haze over the Charles River, where the dinghies darted over and back between Longfellow and Harvard bridges. News bulletins reported that forest fires in Quebec had caused smoke to drift across Maine, New Hampshire, and south to Boston where the smog smothered the city's sky-line. But the sky was translucent in East Walpole, the ribs of sunshine glancing off a yellow van that blazed the slogan, *Grab a Peggy Lawton*—an enticement to purchase the famous New England fudge brownie and oatmeal cookie that have been manufactured in the town for six decades.

Here the writer Mary Lavin was born a full century ago, and passed the first nine years of her life. She was the only child of Irish parents—Nora Mahon from Athenry, County Galway, and Tom Lavin of Frenchpark, County Roscommon—and an intuition that her parents' union was not a happy one would later quiver through the writer's intensely personal and autobiographical fiction.

Mary's mother, Nora, "a classic beauty" and eldest of twelve children, was born into an Athenry family of "small-town merchants who sold coal, seeds and guano as well as tea, sugar and spirits." She passed on to her daughter memories of summer strolls around the rampart walls enclosing her home town, and winter evenings of piano music and family sing-songs. Of her father, Mary said, "his hair was black as the devil's ..... everything about him was black." Tom Lavin and Nora Mahon first met on a transatlantic ship in 1908, he making the trip back to Ireland to buy horses for his employer, Charles Bird, she returning from a visit to her grand-uncle pastor in Waltham. It would be three years before the pair married from the Waltham parochial house and settled in East Walpole. From the beginning, however, Nora Lavin was determined to make the crossing back to Ireland, never to return to America.

I amble along East Walpole's drowsy main street, where a man paints a brilliant white fence at the front of his house, and barbeque odours of charcoal and seared meat float from the back garden. It was on this street that the Lavin family lived, and where Mary attended the Bird School, developed her reading tastes with the guidance of town librarian, Miss Childs, and learned to recite *Hiawatha*. I reach the brow of the hill at the town's edge where a metal railing marked off the wooded area that is *Francis William Bird Park*, Mary Lavin's childhood playground. The Bird estate sloped down to the shores of the Neponsett River, across which was the mill where Tom Lavin worked.

I enter the park through tan and charcoal stone pillars, pass a couple strolling with a child in a white dress decorated in a vivid strawberry pattern, and saunter in the shade of the oak trees. Here, a century ago, a small girl with black hair was thrilled by parkland, flowers and water, later writing: "I used to lean along a tree that grew out over the river ... and look down through the gray leaves at the water flowing past below, and I used to think it was not the stream that flowed, but me, spread-eagled over it, who flew through the air! Like a bird! That I'd found the secret!"

In October 1921, as an Irish Government delegation left Dublin to travel to London for the negotiations that would end with the Anglo-Irish Treaty, Tom Lavin gave in to Nora's pleading and booked a transatlantic passage for his wife and daughter; he would return to Ireland later. The transition from America to Athenry is woven into Mary Lavin's autobiographical story, "Lemonade," narrated through the eyes of the young girl Maudie. The night before mother and daughter set sail, the trunks and boxes were ready, "strapped and corded with new white rope," the parlour crowded with visitors as her father opened bottle after bottle of whiskey to his wife's disapproval. Mother and daughter sailed cabin class on the *SS Winefriedian*, and the sea entered into the child's feelings as a powerful emotion—"a lonely thing," that would be fictionalised in a child looking out from a ship "spellbound by that great stretch of water that separated me from my father".

Mary Lavin's first glimpse of Ireland was the flashing of a lighthouse light through the ship's porthole, misted over with breath. Then it was on to Clare junction by train and by sidecar to Athenry where the Mahon house at first appeared magical with its red-papered corridors, stained glass windows, glowing lights, and an endless supply of lemonade from the family grocery downstairs. Mother and daughter would spend the next eight months living with Nora's family in Athenry before settling in Dublin. The fiction writer would extract the lemonade image from that period to connect for the child the worlds of her absent father in East Walpole, her mother's Athenry family home, and the child's early awareness of death in the friary cemetery where the brother of her new friend, Sadie, lay buried. The dead child's mother had placed a bottle of lemonade on his grave.

Mary Lavin carried the childhood experiences of East Walpole, the transatlantic crossing to Ireland, and the months spent in Athenry, through to adult life and into her creative work, extracting from these memories while exploring and reflecting the patterns of these experiences in her writing. Idyllic parkland moments and childhood days wrapped in a father's love are woven into her fiction: "Perhaps there were times when she had a surplus of it [happiness]—when she was young, say, with her redoubtable father, whose love blazed circles around her, making winter into summer and ice into fire." The unhappy union of Mary Lavin's parents bubbles constantly beneath the surface of the writing, frequently breaking through its skin. In the story "Happiness," written over a half-century after Mary Lavin left East Walpole and narrated through the eyes of the unnamed daughter of widow, Vera Traske, Lavin's most autobiographical character reflects on her parents' relationship through the eyes of her child: "Certainly we knew that in spite of his lavish heart our grandfather had failed to provide our grandmother with enduring happiness. He had passed that job on to Mother. And Mother had not made to good a fist of it, even when father was living and she had him—and later, us children, to help."

In future years when there was an onslaught on the writer's own happiness after the 1953 death of her first husband, she—like Vera Traske— would find solace walking "through the woods and along the banks of the river, where she tried vainly to find peace." The grieving widow, Vera, while staying with friends in France, took night swims after the coastguard had left, as her three daughters watched in a frenzy as she moved out of sight in a place where "wave and sky and mist were one, and the grayness closed over her."

The children waited, staring out, damp hands locked together, until they saw "an arm lift heavily up and wearily cleave down" and their mother reappeared into view.

The garden was the space where Vera could rest and find peace, the area where she imaginatively foresees her own dying, "bent close to the ground," her hands "grubbing in the clay," as her family "were waiting for her to come in before we called an end to the day." For four hours Vera battled death, her world "a whirling kaleidoscope of things which only she could see," until finally she let out a sigh, closed her eyes, and "her head sank so deep into the pillow that it would have been dented had it been a pillow of stone."

The shadows are lengthening as I depart William Bird Park to a chorus of bird song, blaring motorbike engines, and lawnmower motors. I pass a row of houses in pastel colours with dark shutters, the gardens sprinkled with wine and purple rhododendron, as groups congregate for summer evening meals. Soon I am on board the 34A bus, leaving East Walpole behind and facing the long stretch of Washington Street back to Boston. Next day I board an Aer Lingus plane at a storm-filled Logan Airport and cross the Atlantic to Ireland through turbulent skies.

Note: 2012 marked the centenary of the birth of Mary Lavin who was born on 10 June 1912 in East Walpole, Massachusetts, USA.

Rita Ann Higgins

GRANDCHILDREN

It's not just feasible at the moment
one daughter tells me.
What with Seamus still robbing banks
and ramming garda vans when he gets emotional
on a fish-free Friday in February.

Maybe the other daughter could deliver.
She thinks not, not at the moment anyway
while Thomas still has a few tattoos to get
to cover any remaining signs that might link him
with the rest of us.

Just now a B52 bomber flies over
on its way from Shannon
to make a gulf in some nation's genealogy.

The shadow it places on all our notions is crystal clear
and for a split second helping
it juxtaposes the pecking order.
Now bank robbers and tattooers
have as much or as little standing
as popes and princes
and grandchildren become another lonely utterance
impossible to pronounce.

Rita Ann Higgins

NO ONE MENTIONED THE ROOFER

for Pat Mackey

We met the Minister,
we gave him buns, we admired his suit.
The band played, we all clapped.

No one mentioned the roofer;
whose overtime was cut
whose undertime was cut
whose fringe was cut
whose shoelaces were cut
whose job was lost.

We searched for his job
but it had disappeared.
One of us should have said,

Hey Minister, we like your suit
have a bun, where are our jobs?
But there was no point
he was here on a bun eating session
not a job finding session.

His hands were tied.
His tongue a marshmallow.

Eoin Bourke

KING UBU

Blind and unwavering indiscipline at all times constitutes the real strength of all free men.

Laughter is born out of the discovery of the contradictory.

ALFRED JARRY

Alfred Jarry's *Ubu Roi* first saw the light of day in the form of a schoolboy prank. When attending the Lycée de Rennes at the age of 15 he joined forces with a classmate to write a lampoon about their unpopular and ineffectual physics teacher, the pompous and obese Félix Hébert, whom they re-christened Père Heb in their scribblings. After several metamorphoses these sketches, originally written to be performed with marionettes, were shaped into the play *Ubu Roi* and performed for the first time at the Théâtre de l'Oeuvre in Paris on the 9th and 10th of December 1896. Appearing on stage before the curtain rose on the dress rehearsal, a pale-faced Jarry, looking like a "circus clown in a white shirt with a huge starched front and an enormous bow-tie" (Keith Beaumont), held a highly bizarre speech in which he invited the audience to see in Monsieur Ubu as many allusions as they wished, "or else a simple puppet—a schoolboy's caricature of one of his professors who personified for him all the ugliness of the world". He concluded his speech by saying that "the action takes place in Poland—that is to say, nowhere." The curtain rose to reveal Ma and Pa Ubu, the latter with a grotesque pinhead and a huge paunch adorned by a spiral. Fermin Gémier, the prominent Comédie Française actor who played Ubu, triggered off a 15-minute riot on uttering the first word of the play: "Merdre!", a distortion of the word "merde" (shit).

On the second evening there was again a riot. The first one had been caused by the audience's offended sense of decorum—you might, after all, use the expletive "shit" in all-male company, but certainly not in the theatre where ladies were present. The second riot happened because of the audience's expectations of how theatre was to represent reality. When Pa Ubu unlocked a prison door in Act III, Scene 5, there was no actual door on stage but rather an actor *playing* a door. Fermin Gémier later recounted that the actor stood on stage and held out his left arm. "I put the key in his hand as if into a lock. I made the noise of a bolt turning, 'creeeeeeak', and turned my arm as if I was opening a door. At that moment, the audience, doubtless finding the joke had gone on long enough, began to shout and storm; shouts broke out on every side, together with insults and volleys of booing. It surpassed everything in my experience." The theatre director, Aurélien Lugné-Poë, dealt with the situation in his own way by bringing up the lights on the auditorium and revealing very respectable members of high society standing on their seats screaming out their own variations of "merde".

The public were not ready for Jarry's anti-illusionistic scenery (painted by his friends Toulouse Lautrec and Pierre Bonnard) showing "doors opening upon fields of snow under blue skies, fireplaces furnished with clocks and swinging wide to serve as doors, and palm trees growing at the foot of the bed so that little elephants standing on bookshelves can browse on them" (Jarry). In the Paris of the fin-de-siécle, realistic theatre had become the expected convention. The plot had to be plausible and coherent, while the stage set was usually like an elaborately furnished living-room with one wall missing. But Jarry would have none of it, neither of "the stupid concern of our modern theatre with verisimilitude" nor with authentic-looking interiors and "the notoriously hideous and incomprehensible objects that clutter up the stage." Nor did he intend for one moment to comply with the expectations of middle-class theatre-goers to be entertained, moved or edified, to relish plays about "the virtues, patriotism and ideals of people who have dined well" (Catulle Mendèz). On the contrary: he set out to jolt, insult and nonplus them "because the public—inert, obtuse, and passive—need to be shaken up from time to time so that we can tell from their bear-like grunts where they are—and also where they stand." Ostensibly a travesty of Shakespeare's bloody drama *Macbeth*, *King Ubu* presents an onslaught of lavatory humour and an orgy of savage greed and brutality. False pathos and lofty rhetoric alternate with Punch-and-Judy slapstick and vulgarity. Jarry builds on the scatological traditions of Rabelais and Swift in recognition of the human body's need to urinate, defecate and copulate as a built-in mechanism of self-parody constantly ironizing Man's claim to dignity and spirituality. In his use of grotesque masks and costumes he also quotes from the tradition of carnival, that medieval pre-Lenten period of madness that still persists in Catholic communities in mainland Europe in which the populace lets its animality hang out for six weeks as compensation for the impending strictures of Lent, in which men dress up as women, women as men and both as devils, popes and monsters, and cavort wildly through the streets, turning the hierarchical order on its head. The grotesque in Philip Thomson's definition presents "a clash between incompatible reactions—laughter on the one hand and horror and disgust on the other", and as such is "an appropriate expression of the problematic nature of existence."

One person in the audience on that night of 10 December 1896—W.B. Yeats—saw it as highly disturbing but perhaps even uncannily appropriate. The performance marked for him the passing of the pursuit of the aesthetic: "After Stéphane Mallarmé," he wrote, "after Paul Verlaine, after Gustave Moreau, after Puvis de Chavannes, after our own verse, after all our subtle colour and nervous rhythm, after the faint mixed tints of Conder, what more is possible? After us the Savage God." But was Jarry's savage and grotesque idiom not better equipped than subtle colours and faint mixed tints to reflect the world that preceded and was to follow the fin-de-siécle? The past century had seen the "Great Nations" of Prussia, Russia and Austria indulging in greed on an epic scale in the gobbling up of Poland. By the time Jarry wrote his play Poland was still "nowhere", the country having been offered up to the despoilers by the Congress of Vienna. Eleven years before his play, the Imperial Nations France, Germany, Great Britain, Portugal, Belgium and Spain (along with a few other nasty little supplicant nations scrambling for their "place in the sun") met in Berlin to carve up Africa between them in the greatest orgy of greed that the world has ever known. With utter contempt for the indigenous populations they divided the cake partially along lines of latitude and longitude for the sake of expediency, cutting through Africa's pattern of a thousand peacefully cohabiting cultures and thus causing strife that still obtains today. The Imperial capitals of Europe drove huge boulevards through their old cities to facilitate the parading of the Imperial armies to the tune of military bands. The nouveau riche, made wealthy by the plundering of their colonial "possessions"(!), occupied the sumptuous apartments along the boulevards, industrialists' spouses waving their scented hankies from their enormous balconies to the furred and feathered cavalrymen prancing past, and called the tastelessly clunky furniture with which they furnished their apartments after the spoliation that had made them rich: "Second Empire". The same Great Nations were already posturing and trumpeting their way to the trenches of Verdun, not to speak of what was to happen throughout Central Europe two decades after that most obscene and brutal of wars. Yes indeed: a Savage God, but not Jarry's, but rather that of his audience. And these tasteless people had the gumption to expect good taste from him? Merdre!

Seen in this light, Jarry's bleak view of humanity is not gratuitous. The obscenity of his dialogues is by no means inappropriate in the face of the obscenity of the Imperial wars, his blasphemous expletives nothing compared to the outrageous blasphemy of bishops blessing tanks, of "Great Nations" presuming that God is on their side and invoking Him to aid them in crushing their enemies, of heads of state exhorting the youth that it is glorious to die for one's Fatherland—and contribute to the economic gain of those who sent them out to die. To make us mindful of the impact that Jarry's play had, one must try to reconstruct the prevailing mood and ethos of the time. One thing is particularly remarkable: Jarry's avantgarde contemporaries and those who were to follow all claimed his play to be either a prime example or a forerunner of their own movements: the Symbolists, the Dadaists, the Surrealists, Antonin Artaud's Theatre of Cruelty as well as the Theatre of the Absurd. Jarry even foreshadowed Brecht's epic theatre in featuring the latter's famous alienation effect: the use of placards to announce scene changes, the interruption of the action by songs, the actors stepping out of his or her role to make announcements to the audience, all in order to counteract the illusionism of conventional theatre. In other words, the erstwhile schoolboy prank had untold reverberations in the world of European theatre. What a pity it had no impact on the people it tried to address. The play was taken off after the two performances mentioned never to be staged again before Jarry's early death.

Michael Gorman

NOR WAS I PRESENT

Nor was I present on the morning
you enquired how long you had left.
Later that night we watched
Leeds play Stuttgart together.
When Cantona turned the game on its head
we laughed about your early preference
for strikers with raw power
like Malcolm Macdonald,
even Clyde Best.

After the game was over
you pointed to the red light
on the coin-operated Solara set
at the foot of the hospital bed
and said: "I think that thing
is using up the money
even when it's turned off."

The late stab at thrift
was the only clue you gave
and I lacked whatever skill
it takes to tell the difference
between someone who is grievously ill
and another of the worried well.

When we were all together in Sligo,
most of us the same, monochrome,
and the County Manager, Mr T.J. McManus
snaked across the town
in his baby-blue Mercedes,
I did not know then
what I know now.
That understated engine conveyed
the noise of low-pitched power,
the capacity to hire and fire.

Michael Gorman

PULLING THE DEVIL BY THE TAIL

Tell me this and tell me
no more, do you think
you'll ever be able
to eke out a living?

On the way to Boot Hill,
his voice failing,
throat raw from radiotherapy,
my father contrived, once again,
to hit the nail firmly on the head.

He might have seen what was coming,
Would have categorised the advance party
in different language.

I know me own know.
These are not the kind of people
You can make out a whole lot.

He was the boy with the bucket
in the corner of a damp field
shouting 'soo' to calves
hiding behind clumps of rushes.
The young man out on a Spring morning
running a pair of greyhounds
along the top of Knocknashee,
returning home in the evening
to his own concoction
a combination of milk, bread and sugar
boiled in the precious ponny.

All of his life, he favoured
the kind of truth that is
non-sinister, unlikely to crop up
in courtrooms or newspapers.

Once on a dark, country road
he came upon an empty Ford Popular
with the engine running.
Crouched under its headlamps,
in the only available light,
a priest was reading his breviary.

And if, by any chance,
the moneymen venture west
and pitch their tents
in the vicinity of Sligo cemetery,
he'll surely rouse them early
and lead them up the aisle
to the headstone of Captain Edward P. Doherty,
the 'brave avenger of Abraham Lincoln'.
And as they stand there,
huddled under umbrellas,
like cattle leaning into bushes
during a shower of sleet,
he'll let them know
that, sooner or later,
everyone gets the rattle,
and he'll chart the halted progress
of a rich man from the town
who ended his days, twisted,
with a round hump on his back
like a dog scraping a pot.

Ruth Quinlan

THE HEALING

It is an upright piano—an old, second-hand Rogers. Two workmen deliver it one Saturday morning. Swathed in rough sacking and twine, it resembles a large, angular mummy. She watches from the safety of the kitchen as the workmen sweat, their muscles bunching as they edge it carefully through the narrow front door. Once past, they wheel it the few feet down the hall on its brass castors.

Her father walks backwards ahead of the men, directing them in as they ease the piano over the last hurdle, the saddle of the living room threshold. The shorter, younger man ducks back out to retrieve the piano stool from the van and sets it down in the middle of the large room, next to the piano. The other man takes out a Stanley knife and slices through the bindings until they start to fall away, revealing a tantalising shoulder of burnished wood. His partner pulls roughly at the sacking, bundling and rolling the coarse material under his arm.

She ventures as far as the living room door and hesitates there, torn between wanting to touch the piano and her wariness of the two strange men. Her forehead is getting itchy again and she rubs surreptitiously at it, trying not to let her father see. He put cream on her eczema this morning and asked her to be a good girl and not scratch it off this time.

The taller man replaces the knife in the back-pocket of his overalls and comes over to her father, waving the other man out the door ahead of him. "Go on ahead there Patrick. I'll be out to the van in a little while." He holds out a delivery docket to her father saying, "There you are now Mr Brown. All ready to go. Will it be yourself playing it?"

"No Jimmy, it's for my daughter, Claire." His eyes flick over to the small figure dithering in the doorway. "I wanted to give her an outlet. She stopped speaking…when my wife…" He falters.

"Ah God, I'm sorry Mr Brown, I didn't want to be dragging last year up again for you," Jimmy interrupts quickly, mortified for making the other man talk about his troubles. "There's no better instrument than the piano. I played a bit of it myself when I was younger. We had one in the house from when my grandmother was living with us, God rest her. None of her talent got as far as me though. Didn't matter how many times the teacher rapped my knuckles, I never could sit still. Pure torture, especially when the rest of the lads were outside in the fields playing ball. Still love to listen to it though. I'm sure she'll be a little star. Won't you, pet?" Jimmy asks, smiling at her.

Such a little scrap of a thing, he thinks. Those red bumps all over her face looked pretty sore too. It wasn't right, a mite like her having to deal with so much.

She ducks her head away and slinks into the corner of the room to face away from them. Jimmy feels even worse now for upsetting the child as well as her father and stands there, awkward.

"Claire, come over and have a look at it. It's yours now," her father coaxes, beckoning her closer.

She shakes her head mutely, dark curls swinging. One of her hands begins working at the side of her light cotton dress, twisting the fabric into a tight knot. The other hand scrabbles in underneath her cardigan sleeve to scratch at her arm. Mr Brown's mouth stiffens into a thin line. Then he sighs and looks back at Jimmy.

"Sorry Jimmy. She's not great around strangers. Give me a minute."

He walks over to Claire and hunkers down beside her. Gently, he turns her towards him, prising her fingers loose. He holds them between his own large palms until she stills.

"Stop Claire, you'll make it bleed again. Will you promise to try and stop now for Daddy?"

She looks up at him with serious blue eyes, glancing over at Jimmy before nodding quickly. Her father releases her hands and then stands to re-join Jimmy by the piano.

"Here's a few quid for yourself and Patrick for delivering it so quickly for us. And for taking care with it." He shakes hands with Jimmy and presses a few notes into his palm.

"Cheers Mr Brown, you're a sound man. I wish her many happy years with it." Jimmy turns and waves at Claire before Mr Brown accompanies him out to the front door.

On her own now with the piano, she stares at it silently for a few minutes. It is in the centre of the room, perpendicular to the living room window. The August sun shines in through the glass, throwing shafts of light that reveal rich tones of copper and russet in the mahogany. Dust motes dance in the warm air around it, like flecks of golden pollen. Outside, she sees her father with Jimmy, walking slowly down the concrete driveway towards the moving van. She hears him asking about Jimmy's brothers and sisters.

The piano is still closed after the move. Tentatively, she lays her palm in the centre of it; the wood is smooth and cool. She runs her hand slowly along the length of the cover, rubbing her fingertips back and forth against the thin brass hinge, enjoying the feel of the small interruption in the sleekness—a simple braille.

Finding the cover lip, she slides her fingers underneath and lifts. She pushes the heavy cover back and it falls against the frame before she can catch it, sending a discordant echo throughout the house. She jumps back, frightened. Her heart races and she has to take a couple of deep breaths to slow it, like her father taught her.

She feels something on her hand and when she looks down she sees a thin trickle of blood. It is only then that she realises that her left hand is still burrowing away at her right arm, clawing at the eczema scabs. With a conscious effort, she stops and uses her sleeve to clean the blood off her hand. She doesn't want her father to see it. He looks sad when he sees her scratching. When he looks like that, it makes her stomach twist in on itself. The cream and black keys look like teeth; the keyboard is a huge mouth, grinning at her. Shyly, she smiles back and comes closer, dragging the piano stool with her.

Settling herself on the stool, her foot kicks something at the base of the piano. Looking down, she sees two brass pedals. One is highly polished from use; the other is dull and slightly dusty. She pushes the shiny pedal with her foot but it slips and the pedal springs back. The whole piano vibrates like a gong, like a massive heartbeat. Intrigued by this noise, she does it again and once more, the piano resonates loudly. Stretching her foot out further, she manages to hold the pedal down and presses a key with one finger. With her foot on the pedal, the single note echoes on and on, dying in tiny increments until she is unsure of whether she still hears it—or whether her ear holds the memory of it. It is the beginning of a first conversation, tentative and exploratory;

it is the most beautiful thing she has heard since her mother stopped singing.

In the summer warmth, her whole body feels raw and prickly. On an impulse, she lowers her head to rest a cheek lightly against the keys. As her weight presses downwards, the sounds of an octave drift gently from the piano. The ivory and ebony keys are soothing against her skin and for a minute, the itching ceases.

Turning her head, she smoothes her curls out of the way and presses her other cheek down. The notes resound, slightly louder and lower, before fading away down the hallway. She imagines them floating upwards with the dust motes, out through the front door and into her mother's flower garden, rising higher and higher until they reach the summer clouds. There, they might make music together, before falling to earth in the next shower. She wonders how it would feel to be drenched in song-soaked rain. From the tiny spaces between the keys, she smells the deep, woody perfume of the piano. Underneath, there is another fragrance, candle and honey-like—beeswax polish. She recognizes it because it is the same as her grandmother's dining-room table.

She wishes she smelled like the piano and not like medicine. She inhales, breathing the scent of it further and further into her lungs until she can take no more. The piano is a now part of her, deep down inside.

Raising her head slightly, she notices the shiny metal lettering on the inside of the cover. The word "Rogers" is written in capital letters on one line and underneath, in smaller letters, "London". London sounds familiar; she thinks she has cousins there.

The heat in the room increases as the sun climbs towards noon. She takes off her cardigan. Resting her forehead against the piano's name, she stretches out both her arms, reaching as far as she can, and lowers her shoulders towards the keyboard. A myriad of notes play simultaneously. The cooling sensation of the keys against her tormented skin is wonderful.

Holding her arms straight, she slides slowly to the right, listening to the notes climbing higher. Then to the left, and they grow deeper. She repeats the action once more and then speeds up. Faster and faster, she moves her arms back and forth across the keys, mighty scales and arpeggios sprawling in her wake. Pressed as she is against the very bones of the piano, the sounds are extraordinary, filling her head until she thinks it will burst. The edges of the keys start to tear at her scabs but she does not notice. The hurt, inside and out, is momentarily forgotten, absorbed by the music all around her. A great chord rings out when she finally stops.

Mr Brown waves goodbye to Jimmy and Patrick as they drive off and walks back up the long driveway. As he approaches, he hears a deafening cacophony from inside, then silence. Rushing towards the living room, he is halted at the door. For a moment, he does not see his seven-year-old daughter in front of him. Instead, he sees the pale figure of his dark-haired wife, spread-eagled across the white sheets of their bed, an empty brown prescription bottle by her hand. He has to grip hard at the doorframe to steady himself. He blinks and sees his daughter, stretched out and bleeding, as if crucified against the wood of the piano. He runs forward to kneel beside her and takes her in his arms, lifting her away from the stool.

"What have you done to yourself Claire?" he asks desperately, clutching her to his chest.

"It's OK Daddy," she whispers.

It is the first time she has spoken in a year and he cries with relief. She strokes his back, her arms leaving small bloodstains on his white shirt.

Pete Mullineaux

MAKING RAIN

I enter the classroom armed with my rainstick—
this is 'creative writing' and we are here to hunt
for words. The walls are already hung with trophies
from earlier forays—some in Irish, English, others
more recent and exotic, and though they are there
to offer encouragement, I'm conscious how even
this modest treasure-trove might loom over apprentice
shoulders at the blank page; inhibit, dazzle.

Let us not look. Instead we will see with our ears
as the clock ticks, a chair squeaks,
voices resound along the corridor; cars go by,
the wind rattles a loose window
and a low hum of the heating system
echoes a communal heartbeat.
As bellies rumble, we have laughter.

We gather around the rainstick, become
ourselves a rain-forest: rubbed fingertips
suggest rustle of wind in leaves… finger snap
pitter-pat, hands slap knees into torrid downpour,
kicking up a storm as feet pound the floor
into hailstones and thunder.

Next step: percussion to mouth sounds—
whispering wind, tongue clicks of drip-drop;
lip-smacking hard rain as bullfrogs
leap from lily pads—we yodel sleet and hail
with ice the size of golf balls!
Now we are a choir.

Conor Montague

from COWBOYS IN INDIA

"C'mon, let's suss out this Taj Mahal."

"Are you completely insane?"

"What? That's what we're here for."

JD looks at me sideways, as if seeing me for the first time. He takes time to gaze at the chaotic little scenes sprinkled all around then turns back to me.

"Are you completely insane?"

I do my best not to be angry at JD for paying that thieving tuk-tuk driver. Now he's giving out to me for standing up to the fucker. I turn and walk to the stiles. JD shakes his head and follows. We pay 100 rupees each, walk through the gates of the Taj Mahal and stand awestruck. All of our hassles and disagreements dissipate into the ambiance of the enclosed space. Very few monuments or attractions live up to their hype. Though we are just inside the gate, and two-hundred metres from the building itself, we know that all the heat and hardship of the past week is vindicated by our arrival into this garden. We sit on a marble ledge at the head of the tree-lined stretch of still reflective water that leads up to the marble mausoleum. Parakeets whistle as they flit between trees, flashes of green and red across the blue dome.

JD informs me that the bench we're sitting on is the same one that Princess Diana posed upon back in 1992. I feign interest, not wanting to spoil the serenity of the place by telling him how little I care about the deceased princess. It's a mistake. He rabbits on about the irony of her posing alone at this, the greatest monument to love on the planet, then opens his *Lonely Planet* guide and embarks on a historical diatribe into my ear. The sun is warm on our backs. Sweet scents waft through the air with brightly coloured butterflies and anger slowly seeps out of me, leaving Sanjog a lifetime away, lost somewhere in the stinking grime outside the walls. I take photos as JD speaks.

"The building was constructed by the Mughal Emperor, Shah Jahan, in memory of his wife of seventeen years, Mumtaz Mahal. She died in 1631, giving birth to their fourteenth child. Fucks sake! Fourteen kids! Catholic

135

blood there somewhere. The heartbroken emperor started building the Taj in the same year and it took twenty-two years to complete. Workers were brought from all over central Asia, a total of twenty-thousand in all. Experts were even recruited from Europe, though the main architect was an Iranian by the name of Isa Khan."

A tiny middle-aged man, with round spectacles and white robe, approaches. He looks like a re-incarnation of Gandhi himself. He tells us that he is a guide, and will gladly show us around for a meagre donation. I tell him that I have a guide and nod towards JD. He bows politely and leaves. His easy manner endears him to me and I call him back. The history will sound more authentic coming from Indian lips.

His name is Gurudas, which he informs us means servant of the guru. We descend steps and stroll along the right side of the dividing watercourse on red sandstone paving. His soft voice complements birdsong as a light breeze rises from the Yamuna River. "You are lucky," he says, "morning not busy." He pauses frequently as we walk, always waiting a few moments before he speaks, as if to absorb the essence of the decorative gardens we pass through. They are set out according to classical Mughal designs, known as *Charbagh*, which consist of a square garden, quartered by watercourses. We stop halfway up, at the *Al-Kawthar*, or "The Celestial Pool of Abundance", to stand at the dead centre of a cross of mirrored water. Gurudas points to a red building at the end of one watercourse.
"That is museum. We look after, no hurry, enjoy sunshine yes?"
The three of us digest the view in all directions, silent and content. Gurudas takes long deep breaths through his pointed nose, inhaling the positive ions that rise from the water as the day heats up. I look at the Taj and visualise thousands of workers furiously building as Shah Jahan watches, each marble block reminds him of his great loss while expressing his undying love. And here it stands, four-hundred and fifty years later. The Mughal Empire long crumbled, British dominion a fading memory, but this beautiful monument to ever-lasting love stands proud and alone in the middle of a shit-hole town, oblivious to the filth, the poverty, transient eras that come and go through the centuries before becoming mere footnotes in history.
JD and Gurudas have ambled half way up the pathway. I catch up as they

climb the steps to the white marble platform that serves as a pedestal for the Taj. Gurudas speaks of the four white minarets that surround the building, one at each corner of the platform. They are purely decorative, as the Taj Mahal is not a mosque, so nobody is called to prayer from them. He points out that the minarets lean slightly outwards, and sure enough, when viewed up close, we can see that he tells the truth. This is in case any of them were ever to fall, to ensure that they would tumble outwards, so as not to damage the Taj itself. There are identical red sandstone buildings on each side, one of which is a mosque, the other built to maintain perfect symmetry. It cannot be used as a mosque as it faces the wrong direction.

To the rear of the platform we look out over the Yamuna River and see the Red Fort across the way, an impressive structure even from this distance. The river is low, a glinting silver thread slowly meandering through a flood-plain of sandy marsh, patrolled by platoons of egrets, herons and storks, all oblivious to the landmarks on either side. As we look across at the fort, Gurudas fills us in on the tragedy of Shah Jahan. Apparently, he intended to build a second Taj Mahal, this one in black marble, to be used as his tomb. Plans were drawn up for this perfect counter-image of the white Taj. However, the Shah's son, Aurangzeb, obviously worried about the steady drain on his inheritance, put a stop to the madness. He overthrew his father and imprisoned him in the Red Fort, where he spent the rest of his days looking out the window of his cell at his wife's tomb. We curse Aurangzeb for depriving us of the pleasure of a black marble Taj Mahal then walk across the platform towards the main building. JD points to red blotches all over the white marble, mementos of countless spitting Indians. Guradas shakes his head resignedly, "Pigs" is all he says before continuing on. The central structure is every bit as impressive close-up as it is from a distance. Perfectly symmetrical, four small domes surround the huge central bulbous dome which crowns perfectly aligned archways which contain finely-cut marble screens through which light is admitted to the interior. The walls are inlaid with thousands of semi-precious stones, arranged in patterns through a process known as *pietra dura*.

The main chamber contains two tombs, which Guradas tells us are false. The authentic tombs—those of Shah Jahan and his wife, Mumtaz Mahal, are in the basement. I'm relieved that Aurangzeb at least had the integrity to place his father's remains in an adjoining tomb to his beloved wife. By all accounts, he acted for the good of the empire. Had his grief-stricken father had his way, the family would have been crippled financially. Future tourist revenues would have been scant consolation to the skint son of a broke emperor.

Guradas howls like a wolf. The sound echoes around the chamber. It gains resonance and timbre as it unfurls and spins along the inside of the dome, before it gradually fades into illusionary distance. He smiles as we exit into blinding light, awed by the time spent within. We look over the gardens for a moment to allow our eyes to readjust then walk down to the museum. Guradas remains outside while we wander half-heartedly through architectural drawings, Mughal swords, and Celadon plates, which JD informs me change colour if poisoned food is placed upon them. We exit to find our guide sitting cross-legged under a tree among the parakeets and starlings. A sacred ibis stands motionless in the shade, black and white plumage and long orange beak contrasting beautifully with green foliage.

We sit in silence beside Guradas on the grass and watch the garden's activities reflected in the water until our world inverts and we ourselves become reflections, mere mirror images of an illusion. The sacred ibis takes flight and breaks the spell. We could stay forever but there's a Red Fort to explore and hunger to be sated. We ask Guradas to accompany us but he declines with a smile. He tells us that he has people to meet, and to only pay 20 rupees for tuk-tuk. He walks us to the gate. We give him 100 rupees for his splendid company and exit to the noise and filth of the outside world. I steal one final wistful glance over my shoulder before being engulfed by touts once again.

Megan Buckley

JANUARY

My frown fiddles with the weather, you tell me;
And so I am to blame for the coming rain.
We watch the lowering cloud outside the window
Move into the branches of the elm, and wait. Sure enough,
Within seconds, a fantastic clatter of pebbles on the roof,
A sandstorm of hailstones roars above our heads,
Those raindrops turned tight and rough. We run to the door
To watch the earth fall from the sky and land at our feet,
A white war-time terrain.

In the afterstorm still, you disappear through that door
To bend across the flowerbed and then the sidewalk, to scrape
the melting shreds into a paper cup. When you return,
you hand me the cupful of white bullets
with the smile of a long-departed conqueror,
of a traveller come home. You smile all that afternoon, as we
nibble the hailstones like popcorn with our iced fingers,
tasting roots and dirt and footprints,
and the rain I birthed by accident.

Gerard Hanberry

EMBERS

When Apollo ordered Mithras to sacrifice a bull
he carried out the task unwillingly, mosaics depict
his face averted. As the bull died the animal became
the moon, Mithras' mantle the starry sky.

From the bull's blood the first corn sprouted,
the first purple grapes. Every other thing sprang
from his seed, except the scorpion.
The scorpion drinks seed and blood.

*

Their days are passed in silences
or set pieces, coming and going,
holding out as best they can,
retreating into props and costumes
and south facing rooms,
ignoring the fact that no one ever calls.

And still they make love,
more in hope then passion,
like two castaways
keeping the signal-fire burning
on the off chance,
taking turns to fan the embers,

to straighten the help sign
built with white stones
along their beach.
Each night the great breakers roll in
to wipe away the footprints,
now his, now hers.

*

The old cartographers were right;
it is possible to drop off the edge of the world
and monsters of the deep exist
exactly where the ancient charts placed them.

*

Spires of pine trees, medieval, here and there on the amber hillside;
silence not yet shattered by traffic on the Strada Aurelia.

She sleeps little in this high-ceilinged room, her fears rustling
like night-creatures in the wood, the air already dry as dead leaves.

Yesterday, a man in the gift-shop smiled but it was not
a stranger's smile she wanted. No, not his, not his.

A great bird, a hawk maybe, rises broad-winged and circles, circles,
white petals curl on the veranda, pearl-shells loose from the patterned wall.

On the bedside table near his sleeping head,
the door-sign in bold lettering—DO NOT DISTURB.

*

Where the ancient river winds
through the scorched earth of Campagna
it's hard to know east from west.
A lizard, throat pulsing in the heat,
clings to a rock, waits, listens,
then slithers for his dusty crevice.

She remains in the Piazza while he climbs
the stairs to the Basilica's great dome.
Higher, higher, slowly winding, a hymn, a chant,
perhaps it's not too late, my love, perhaps it's not too late.
Then the city spreads before him, the curving
colonnades of St. Peter's, elliptical, like a claw.

He sees her far below among the wandering tourists,
standing near the fountain, tiny, unmistakable.
He wants to call out. The sky is marble blue and
beautiful; they were right to come. But she moves,
crossing by Nero's obelisk, its shadow long and black
across the square, a tail, its sharp point the sting.

*

They have arrived at the ruins of Ostia.
He thumbs the guidebook in the shade,
cap pulled low against the blaze of white sunlight,
she prowls the edges, making her own way

through empty courtyards, the tilt and stagger
of columns, to the still of an amphitheatre where
she sits, knees drawn up, watching three wild cats
move away over the steps like wishes softly rebuffed.

In the cool of Mithras' Temple they share Casareccio
bread and Chianti, splashing wine into plastic cups,
red droplets falling on the mosaic floor, on the scorpion
and across the bull, his neck stretched for the blade.

By the Via Ostiense they sit apart in deepening shadow,
down this ancient road an Empire marched,
no clang of legions now, no throb of *seed and blood*,
just the dry crackle of their plastic cups.

Then faint through the ages and the gathering twilight,
drawn perhaps by their dismay, their defeat, come faded
sounds, a woman sobbing, a door being nailed and shuttered,
the last bundled cart creaking up the road for Rome.

Gerard Hanberry

TRIBETOWN

for Adrian Frazier

Days when the soft mists wait out at sea
and the sun comes to fill this place with jigs and reels
drawing the chill from the old limestone

youth sprawls in tribal circles
with banjos, drums and didgeridoos,
strange rhythms picked up on walkabout.

Here the world finds space to draw its breath,
and the truce holds, while the river
tumbles by like a festival parade.

In the Square the sculpted sails
stand frozen in their hooker's curve
and nobody is waiting for the spell to break.

Moya Roddy

SEAGULL

When Rachel overheard the Head saying Miss McCarthy was on "probation" she wondered what the word meant. Everyone in third class liked Miss McCarthy. She was the only teacher who never asked you to sit up straight or shouted if you looked out a window. Sometimes she told stories between lessons. Today she'd told them one about St Francis of Assisi and the birds. At lunchtime some of the boys said the story was sissy. Rachel knew that meant something only girls liked.

On her way home Rachel tried to dream up an idea for her composition. Miss McCarthy hadn't given them a title, just told them to write about something that interested them. Passing Doran's, she stopped and looked at the sweets, pressing her face against the shop window. Her breath left a haw mark and as she drew a heart in it she could hear the sound of voices, yelling and shouting. Quickly, she put an arrow through the heart then racing up the road she saw a gang of boys milling and pushing in front of an empty house with a big "For Sale" sign in the garden. Rachel hung back, watched.

"There it is!" a boy with red hair screamed.

"There, there!"

"Behind the bush. It's moving."

"It's wounded!" someone squealed. "Shoot again!"

One of the bigger boys lifted something thin and black, aimed.

Rachel knew instantly it was a pellet gun although she'd never seen one.

"Stop, don't!"

"Shut up," the boy said. "You're just a girl."

Everyone laughed.

He raised the gun a second time.

"Sissy," Rachel screamed. "Sissy!"

The boy hesitated. Seizing her chance, Rachel darted towards the injured seagull, picked it up.

"Can't kill it now," she taunted, trying to cover it with her cardigan. The bird, larger than it had seemed, flapped and squawked, its heart thrumming like a sewing machine. A wing grazed her face.

"We saw it first. Let it go," the redheaded boy ordered.

"It's not yours," the one with the gun menaced.

"Babies, that's all yous are, trying to kill a poor seagull." The bird pecked at her, squawked even louder.

"Ha, ha, ha!" Some of the boys began to laugh, holding their stomachs in an exaggerated way.

Rachel searched their faces, trying to figure out what could be so funny. "Shit all over you, dirty thing."

Looking down, she noticed a skitter of birdshit on her skirt.

"Serves you right, serves you right," they jeered.

"Keep your old seagull," the boy with the gun scoffed. "It'll die anyway. C'mon. There's rats over the back."

Flapping their arms and squawking, the boys ran off backwards. Rachel out-stared them, then, as soon as they were out of sight, she held up the cradled seagull which had gone quiet.

"Jesus, Mary and Joseph!" Rachel's mother's shrieked. "What have ye got there? What's the matter with it?"

"Some boys shot it with pellets. They were going to kill it."

"What did you butt in for? Which boys?"

"I'm going to look after it." She held out a hand. "Look, there's blood."

"Ugh, take it out of the kitchen. Quick!"

"But Mammy ..."

"Out, out, we don't want germs. And wash your hands."

"Can't we put it in a box in the shed?"

"Alright, alright. Your daddy'll be home soon, we'll ask him what to do."

"Can I give it something to eat?"

"In the shed, the shed. I'll bring something out."

Rachel offered the bird dry bread then bread soaked in milk but the seagull showed no interest. She murmured encouragement in what she hoped was bird language, stroked its back lightly, aware of a cage of bones beneath the feathers. All of a sudden the bird reared, the cage expanding beneath her hand, wings extending out like fans. Springing to her feet, she ran to the shed door, flung it open. "Fly," she urged pointing to the sky, "fly." The bird tottered a few steps then a glazed look crept into its eyes and the outspread wings collapsed. Rachel blinked away a tear. Maybe sleep would make it better. It's what her mother said when she was sick. As she hummed a lullaby the seagull's eyes stayed open, gazing at her, blindly.

Rachel heard the crunch of footsteps then a shadow blotted out the light. Looking up, she saw her daddy.

"We'll make it better, won't we?" she asked as he hunkered down beside her.

Her father opened his eyes wide the way he did when he was thinking about something important but said nothing.

"Take it to the vet? Why?" Rachel asked as her mother hovered in the shed doorway. The seagull hadn't moved since tea-time, lay curled in a corner of the box, making tiny, whimpery sounds.

"Your daddy thinks it's best. The vet'll know what to do. That's his job, looking after sick things."

Remembering the story Miss McCarthy had told them about St Francis, Rachel nodded. "You'll be alright now," she whispered to the sick bird.

Rachel sat in the waiting room making herself read the advertisements on the walls but a lot of the words were difficult. What could her mother and the vet be talking about in the next room? At last, the door opened and her mother beckoned her.

"It's very sick," the vet explained, his hands busy with a small bottle of pale liquid. "We could give it something to put it to sleep. Wouldn't that be nice?"

His voice dripped like treacle.

"You don't want it suffering, do you?" her mother asked.

Rachel shook her head.

"Don't worry. It won't feel a thing, and then it'll go for a long, long sleep," the man assured her over his shoulder.

As the needle went in Rachel closed her eyes.

"All done," she heard him say, then a swish of water as he washed his hands. "I'll dispose of it later."

Rachel's heart somersaulted. "You killed it," she screamed, flying at the man. "You killed it!"

"Don't be making a show!" her mother hissed, pulling her away.

Rachel's heart pounded. She wanted to scrape the vet's eyes out. Kill him.

"There, there. She didn't understand, that's all." "That'll be thirty euros," he added.

"You did it for money," Rachel shouted. "Money! At least the boys were having fun."

Rachel pulled the duvet over her head. If only she'd understood putting the bird to sleep meant killing it. A taste of sick rose in her throat. What use were stupid words! They could only tell you what happened. They could never get to the feeling.

Writing the essay Rachel pretended the bird had been injured accidentally. Bad words weren't allowed so she left out the bit about birdshit and instead of the visit to the vet she put in a long paragraph about birds in general. All the rest was true.

Mary O'Malley

THE DATE

It's never as you expect it to happen.
The woman, late on new year's night
Waits in the house on the Fontanka.
The one has not arrived to whom
She can offer Russia. She is alight
With her own suffering, a gilded icon
With a slash of red lipstick. She writes
In the air, on her tongue, on ice. She lights
Candles, lays out the crystal for wine.

She does this because a poet
Does not give up when the expected
Hero lets her down. She drinks alone
And sits on, working until the dawn.
Of the hero, his missed chance
Nothing is recorded, but absence
Burning like an icicle lamp.

Hugo Kelly

THE FACE IN THE WALLPAPER

That summer there is something wrong in the house. The boy wanders from room to room searching through the shadows for a reason. The Face-in-the-Wallpaper smiles then sneers and the boy has to quickly run away. The Face-in-the-Wallpaper knows everything. It knows that the boy would love a watch.

"What do you want a watch for? You can't even tell the time," it sneers.

"Oh yes I can," the boy lies, but The-Face-in-the-Wallpaper doesn't hear him.

In the sitting room the delta of meeting rivers on the cracked ceiling holds the boy's attention. If he closes his eyes he can hear their Amazonian roar. The diamonds that live in the carpet dance around him if he stares without blinking. The stairs to the attic is dark and there is a smell of old clothes and of another age that seems less bright than his own. But the skylight in the attic is his friend. Its rich light performs a cross-section on the darkness inside, revealing its dusty entrails.

In August before anyone even noticed their early appearance, he had gone to the horse chestnut tree by the church and collected the spiked, snot green fruit and brought them to the attic. There he left them on the ledge beside the skylight until the sun and the warmth opened the green skin to reveal the wooden, shining pearls inside. The white dot is an eye. Their touch is firm, yet soft, perfect. They are the meaning of newness. He saves the best one to show to Mr. Canning.

Mr. Canning lives next door and runs the American Bar. He has postcards tacked to the wall beside the upright bottles of spirits. Blue skies gleam, arc shaped golden beaches curl, tiny bikinied women swim about dog-eared edges. They are his window into the world he says and he asks people to send them to him. And so they do: from Majorca and Florida and Benidorm and Corfu.

The boy loves the bar and its certainties. In here there are no faces or no shadows, only the comfortable company of men. There are the red, foamy seats that gently fart if you move too quickly. Then the smoky, sweet smell laced with the undertow of paraffin from the heater. Pictures of policemen and American presidents and boxers posing in white tights cover the walls. High on the shelf, the brown colour television throws out images of horse-racing and never-ending news programmes. The stuffed fox with its rusty coloured fur and tack-like teeth keeps guard above the bar. Best of all there is a round clock that you don't need to wind.

Today Mr Canning reads the paper carefully. The boy counts to one hundred in fives for him. The man nods after each number.

"Good," he murmurs when he finishes. "Now what's the capital of France?"

"Paris," the boy replies.

"Do you hear what the lad knows and him only seven?"

The men look up, momentarily distracted.

"He's a bright one."

"And tall for his age too."

Benjy the drunk is sitting on a high stool. He slowly raises his head showing off his unshaven face. His skin is white and sweaty like raw potato.

"The scholar speaks," he says in a slurred voice.

He laughs then and the boy doesn't like this man's laugh. He is frightened of Benjy who roams the streets like a predatory ghost.

The boy peers at the clock.

"It is five o'clock," he guesses.

Mr. Canning turns the page of the paper.

"That's right," he says. "But that's an easy one."

"Give me another pint," Benjy says.

"Take your time," says Mr Canning.

"You take your time," Benjy replies. "I need a drink."

Mr Costello ignores him.

"God you know what I think it's going to rain," someone says.

A tap drips. A man coughs. The boy takes a piece of ice in his mouth and crunches it. Drops splinter across the windows. Rain is an inevitable as silence.

Benjy suddenly shouts out, "All I want is a bloody drink."

Everyone lifts their head in surprise at the raised voice.

The proclamation is too much and the man slips from the stool and sprawls slowly to the ground. He grunts with effort as he pulls himself up.

"You bloody fool," Mr Canning says. "You'll injure yourself yet."

"Give me a baby Powers'," Benjy says.

"I won't. You can find somewhere else to hang around until your bus."

Benjy stares at Mr Costello. At first he looks worn and weary. But then his face grows sharp and he bares his brown stained teeth.

"How's the Missus?" he asks. He laughs then. An ugly laugh. "She hasn't been seen for a while."

There is silence in the bar except for the ponderous ticking of the clock. The boy looks around all the faces. They are so still as if everyone is holding their breath.

"Get out," Mr Canning hisses.

Benjy smirks, picks up his shopping bag, nearly falling over as he does so. But the sly grin still remains.

"Give her my regards anyways," he says.

Slowly he turns, staggers out the door. The men in the bar return to their drinks. The door flaps to a close but the bar does not feel the same.

"I didn't know you have a wife," the boy says.

Mr Canning does not hear him, instead he stays looking at the closed door. Eventually he speaks wearily, "Go home lad and play with your toys while you still can. Your questions will be the death of me."

The boy doesn't want to go home. He thinks of a funny joke.

"Did you hear about the dirty egg?" he says, "it went around with its yoke hanging out."

Mr Canning opens the door and points out. The boy trails through it despondently. Home to the shadows.

Later the boy asks his mother does Mr Costello have a wife. But she doesn't reply to him. He doesn't feel like asking the question again.

In bed the sandstorm comes early. He stays under the blankets until he begins to sweat. Time passes and the boy puts his head out. The Face-in-the-Wallpaper is asleep. The sand storm is gone. He thinks about Mr Costello and his mysterious wife. He wonders about all the things he doesn't know or understand. In time the boy sleeps.

He is woken early by the soft licks of the brush outside his window. It is the man who sweeps the streets. Each day he brushes away the darkness letting the morning light in. If the boy looks out the man is a matchstick silhouette against the inky morning with his long hinged arms that end in yard-brush and shovel. He moves these wooden limbs with a soft skill pulling the sleepy residue of the streets into the width of his shovel palm. Then with a rattle, everything is thrown into his little trolley bin. On he creaks, the street a tinge brighter in his trail.

Outside everything lies strange and vulnerable. The houses stand shivering and bleary-eyed though a soft pink appears as occasional lights shine through curtains. A car drifts by, its engine giving a throaty morning cough. A bike clips along the road, its trim wheels braking, then with a slow yawn speeding up again as the slight hill takes it. A brisk walker prompts you with his clipped bank-official walk. Then silence falls again except for the soft whispers of the yard brush. Wake up it says. Wake up. Wake up. The Face-in-the Wallpaper is still asleep. The boy gets up before it wakes.

This morning he has a day off school and nobody pays him any attention. His mother sits and listens to the radio. Then turns it off when the music comes on. His father goes to work. The silence falls again. The Face-in-the-Wallpaper follows him from room to room, appearing on each wall.

"In the wa-ay. In the wa-ay," it chants.

The boy leaves the house for the brightness of the street.

He leans against the wall and shoots passers by through his fingers. Mr Kelly across the street takes one to the chest and drops like a ton of bricks. He sharpens a lollypop stick. He looks for something to stab. Nothing. Nothing at all.

The American is still closed. The navy blinds block the windows. He wants to see Mr Costello. Yesterday had been strange and he will not mention his wife again. Sulkily he pushes at the door. To his surprise it is unlocked and opens at his touch. He sticks his head inside, inhaling the stuffy sweet odour that now clings to the bar. It is dark and dim like a church.

He lets himself in and the street recedes into the background. It feels cold and there is no comfortable glow of heat and company. To his horror he discovers that shadows live in here as well. The toilets hiss and throw out their bitter, pissy smell.

From above the bar the fox looks down at him. Its brown stained teeth open in an unpleasant grin.

"Well hello," it says, "What do we have here? A juicy, tasty little boy. Mmmmm."

Its legs tense. Is it going to jump at him?

The boy steps back and then glances at the mirror that points to the scullery hatch. To his surprise he can see the back of Mr Costello's head above the sink. He realises that the man hasn't heard him enter. Mr Canning's head is slightly bent as if he is praying or lost in thought. The boy knows he should say something but he stays quiet, afraid to disturb the man.

"Shhhs," says the fox, "watch this. It's quite a show."

Mr Costello rubs his forehead and grimaces. Then he utters a soft sigh as he bends down and picks something up. It takes the boy a confused moment but he recognises the long dull silver barrel of the shotgun that Mr Costello once used for hunting. For a moment he wants to laugh as if he thinks that Mr Canning is playing with the gun but instead the fox pins him with his sly, green eye.

"Do you know what's happening? Go ask the Face-in-the-Wallpaper and it will tell you what's happening. It knows everything."

The boy is breathing heavily. He looks again at the mirror as Mr Canning lifts the gun and places it in his mouth. Beside the mirror the postcards glow an eerie blue. *Greetings from Torremolinos.*

Mr Costello tilts his shoulders as if making a great effort. A muscle twitches in his neck.

"Run," says the fox. "Run as fast as you can."

The boy turns and his heel grinds on the stone floor. There is a tic movement in Mr Canning's head and the mirror now fills with his pale face as he turns to investigate the sound.

The boy has the door open and is gone. The sudden brightness of the street consumes him. The Angelus bells rings out to say it is midday. For a moment he is surprised that people are still walking about and that cars speed by down the street. He runs to the river to look for sprats but he is unable to stay still long enough to see any.

The next day his mother takes him to Cronin's and buys him a watch. Time has a meaning now. Every second that goes by means that you are a second older. The Face-in- the-Wallpaper clicks its teeth.

"You've a watch now and you're growing up. So now tell me: what was Mr Canning doing?"

But the boy shakes his head and ignores him. Later he goes into the American and shows it to Mr Canning. The bar is warm and full of gentle conversation again. Above the bar the fox stays rigid, looking into some dim horizon. Mr Canning as always is reading the newspaper.

"Look at my new watch. It's a Timex," the boy says.

Mr Costello peers down at it.

"God I thought there were enough clocks and watches in the world," he says.

It is a strange comment but he gives the boy a packet of crisps. Still the boy doesn't stay long. His new watch tells him that soon it will be six o'clock and that his tea will be in an hour. He has just time to go to the river and try and catch sprats with his net. Someday he hopes that he will catch a fish. On the way the Angelus bell rings from the church. It is either two minutes early or his watch is two minutes slow. He doesn't know which and that worries him.

Vincent Woods

A NOTE AND POEMS FOR ADRIAN

The glint is what I love, ever since that first sight
on campus, those eyes of yours so bright and curious.
Alert as George Moore's Carra-blue eyes,
the lake lapping of a chill winter's day.
The first time I saw Manet's portrait of Moore
I wished I'd known that pale ginger man.
You helped me know him, your great house of a book
bringing Moore and Moore Hall, Paris, London,
Mayo and the worlds within his worlds
to vivid life. And to light and understanding
the world of Albert Nobbs, 'the finest story
ever told heard in Ballinrobe'; the crossing
of lines, boundaries, norms as only Moore
could have conjured and crossed. You are a wonder
of our western world, your periscope-playbill
rolled and applied to right eye the better to see
the action on stage and the detail of the big picture.
Always looking, always searching behind the surface,
forever questing and questioning, you sharpen
all our vision. And the laugh, your infectious
bursts of glee, that rare and fearless delight in life.
You set laughter to our days. You,
the girls and Cliodhna walking in Galway in summer,
the canal water silver and calm.
Here for you a song text, (I hope
Mary McPartlan will sing it one day),
and a few small poems of love and lust.
From the deep heart of friendship.

Vincent Woods

VALENTINE AND ROSE

Valentine loved Rose
They ran away from town
They were seventeen
They married in Las Vegas
Rose's father followed them
He shot Valentine
Who died in Rose's arms

Valentine and Rose

Stand up for love—
At every turn
Don't let them kill it
Don't let them shoot it down

Mohammad loved Omar
They slept out on the roof
They were seventeen
The moon was very bright
A jealous neighbour watched
She ran to the Mullahs
They killed them in the square

Mohammad and Omar

Stand up for love
Don't watch it die
Don't let them plant a seed of hate
In any girl or boy

Stand up for love

Rose and Valentine
Have a beautiful young son
The apple of their eye
Her father loves him

Mohammad and Omar
Were married in the square
The sun shone bright
Their neighbours blessed them
Stand up for love
For miracle
Rose and Valentine
Mohammad and Omar

Don't let them kill love

Vincent Woods

MEXICAN ROULETTE

It was a close call,
hard to know
which way to swing
that night.
Mexico-city party:
She was beautiful,
Smart as could be,
But there was something
Edgy, too watchful,
This feeling that she'd
Want your skin and soul
There and then.
We hovered, wary
Knowing we could go for it,
And I can't remember
How the dance began
But suddenly I saw you staring,
Smiling, young,
Who'd not give in?—
Your grace and generosity
Filled the night and morning:
Your down-at-heel runners
Untied as you wrote the note,
Sitting on the edge of the bed:
The note I still have somewhere,
In Spanish, on green paper:
'Frutas, flores, noche y sudor
Amigo, placer mi almapara siempre'

Irina Ruppo Malone

THE IRISH REVIVAL AND THE END OF DAYS: GEORGE MOORE AND HENRIK IBSEN

This chapter from Irina Ruppo Malone, *Ibsen and the Irish Revival* (Palgrave Macmillan, 2010) is reproduced with permission of Palgrave Macmillan.

George Moore's literary relationship with Henrik Ibsen was in the early 1900s a matter of public interest. At least James Joyce must have assumed so when he wrote 'The Day of the Rabblement', a pamphlet which he made sure was delivered to Moore's doorstep and which derided the work of the leaders of the Irish Literary Revival. Joyce conceded that Moore's early novels had some originality but claimed that 'his new impulse has no kind of relation to the future of art'. By contrast, the artist of the future would follow in the footsteps of Ibsen and 'carry on the tradition of the old master who is dying of Christiania'.[i] Yet Joyce's representation of Moore as an antithesis to Ibsen was unfair. In 'In the Clay' and 'The Way Back', two stories from *The Untilled Field* (1903), and their 1931 retelling 'Fugitives', Moore parodies and examines the plot of *When We Dead Awaken*, the play that attracted Joyce's unreserved enthusiasm in 1900.[ii] What's more, Moore turns Ibsen's last play into the judgement day of the Irish Revival, contextualising several core issues of *When We Dead Awaken* in relation to the movement.

Moore had been a champion of Ibsen since he saw *Ghosts* in Paris in 1890. As a founding member of Joseph T. Grein's Independent Theatre, a theatrical society dedicated to the staging of Ibsen's plays, Moore was at the centre of the 1890s controversy over the alleged immorality of Ibsen's works. In 1903 and 1904, Moore and Edward Martyn assisted with amateur Dublin productions of, respectively, *A Doll's House* and *Hedda Gabler*. Yet Moore probably impacted Irish attitudes to Ibsen more powerfully in his role as a founder of the Irish Literary Theatre in 1899. Moore and Martyn are highly likely to have contributed to W. B. Yeats's decision to use Ibsen's name to promote the newly founded Irish Literary Theatre. In several articles and speeches made in 1899, Yeats shifted some historical facts to suggest that in drawing their inspiration from Irish mythology and folklore, he, Edward

Martyn, and Moore were following in the footsteps of Ibsen.[iii] The author of *The Vikings at Helgeland* and *Peer Gynt*, as well as *A Doll's House* and *Ghosts*, Ibsen embodied the two conflicting strands of the Irish Dramatic Revival: the romantic nationalist and the dramatic realist or, in other words, the idealist and the anti-idealist approach to writing.

One of the rare mentions of Ibsen's name in Moore's fiction occurs in 'Fugitives', the last story of *The Untilled Field*. A rakish writer, Harding, tells the Irish sculptor Rodney of his meeting with his former model Lucy Delaney. The girl has run away from Ireland to start a stage career. Harding tries to help and takes her to one of London's theatres, but the manager is busy; soon the conversation turns to Ibsen and the possibility of 'getting the public to see a good play', and Harding realizes the futility of his project. [iv]

'Fugitives' is the last story in the 1931 edition of *The Untilled Field*. It is a reworking of two 1903 stories, 'In the Clay' and 'The Way Back'. The narrative is set around 1900, judging from the reference to the Boer War in 'The Way Back'. It was in that year that Ibsen's *When We Dead Awaken* was first published in English. The mention of Ibsen in 'Fugitives', therefore, might indicate Moore's acknowledgement of the similarity of the subject matter of his story and Ibsen's last play: both deal with the relationship of a sculptor and his model. In both texts, the protagonist's name is assonant with Rodin—Rubek in Ibsen, Rodney in Moore. [v]

What Rubek experiences with Irene, and Rodney with Lucy is a perfect communion of minds, in which the model lives for the emerging masterpiece guessing every need of the artist. At the end, the woman is rejected; in Ibsen's play, Irene perceives that Rubek thinks of her as a mere episode in his artistic career and vanishes from his life. And Rodney, in Moore's story, refuses to take Lucy with him as he prepares to leave Ireland, because, as he realizes in the earlier version, 'he would have to look after her till the end of this life. This was not his vocation.' [vi] The beautiful clay image is also altered. In Ibsen's play Rubek finds his vision of the sculpture of the Resurrection Day challenged by the disappearance of the model. Instead of figuring it as 'a young unsullied woman … awakening to light and glory without having to put away from her anything ugly or impure', Rubek creates a group figure: 'men and women with dimly suggested animal faces' swarm from 'the bursting earth'; and in the foreground appears a mournful figure of the artist himself, who is unable to extricate himself from the ground. [vii] In Moore's story, the statue is turned into a lump of clay. Two little boys, the brothers of the model, have heard a priest denounce her to her parents. Without quite understanding the nature of their sister's guilt or the priest's anger, they steal into the studio and break the statue. Rodney feels 'like he could never do sculpture again' (292), echoing Rubek who has become a mere craftsman after completing his only masterpiece.

According to Errol Durbach, Ibsen's play 'investigates … that specifically Romantic attitude to art as creative solution to life's dilemma, a substitute religion in which a god-like creator locates the redemptive hopes of a now effete Christian dispensation.' [viii] This play might well have struck a chord with Moore, who confessed himself, in *Hail and Farewell*, to be the messiah of Ireland called to deliver the land from the empty dogma of Catholicism and awaken it into personality—'personal love and personal religion, personal art, personality for all, except God.' [ix] Yet this new religion must have its sacrifices, and Ibsen's play that, in Durbach's words, measures the 'promise of personal and cultural redemption … against the humanity that must be sacrificed to the ideal' [x] anticipates Moore, who writes in *Hail and Farewell* how he was asking himself 'again and again whether he was "capable of sacrificing brother, sister, mother, fortune, friend, for a work of art."' [xi] Like *When We Dead Awaken*, 'Fugitives' explores the consequences of the artist's rejection of humanity through the inversion of the Pygmalion and Galatea myth.

When after years of estrangement the two meet again, Rubek tries to explain to Irene that he did love her but 'the superstition took hold of me that if I touched you, if I desired you with my senses, my soul would be profaned so that I should be unable to accomplish what I was striving for.' But Irene scorns him for putting 'the work of art first—then the human being' (372). Irene is obsessed with the idea that she is dead and that Rubek's statue is her child, the only legacy of her empty life. 'I hated you', she tells the artist, 'because you could stand there so unmoved'. The following dialogue ensues:

Rubek: Unmoved? Do you think so?
Irene:—at any rate so intolerably self-controlled. And because you were an artist and an artist only—not a man ... But the statue in the wet, living clay, that I loved—as it rose up a vital, human creature, out of those raw shapeless masses—for that was our creation, our child. Mine and yours. (411-2)

The high romanticism of Irene and Rubek reverberates in Moore's comic prose; this is how the artist's predicament in relation to the sexual attraction of the model is described in Moore's story:

The word tomorrow chilled his ardour, so far away did it seem from Lucy, like centuries, and he wished that he could sleep all day, for how the time would pass without her he did not know … he did not care to see other sculpture, and dared even to breathe to himself: 'All I see is dry and insipid compared to what I am doing from Lucy!' … he went to bed hoping he would sleep the time away. But his desire to be at work again on his statue of the Virgin and Child was so great that he slept hardly at all. Lucy was a little late … but he forgot his loss when she had taken the pose, and many days passed in the same excitement, the same exaltation, till one morning she arrived wheeling a perambulator. (289-90)

The play on the words 'excitement' and 'desire', the frequent mention of the word 'bed' culminates in the unexpected image of the woman with a pram — a literal transfiguration of Ibsen's idea of the woman thinking of the work as a child and thus proclaiming the importance of her contribution and the wrong done to her by the artist's neglect of her body. (The child in Moore's story is discovered to be Lucy's baby brother whom she has thoughtfully brought along to pose as the infant Christ.)

Much of the power of *When We Dead Awaken* lies in the comic debasing of the reunion of Rubek and Irene through the developing relationship between Maja, Rubek's clever, vivacious and much patronized prize wife, and Ulfheim the bear hunter. The latter couple, far more interested in the joys of the body than works of art, were described by Bernard Shaw as the man and woman of the Stone Age. [xii] According to Shaw, Ibsen's play asks the following questions: 'What is there to choose between those two pairs? Is the cultured gifted man less hardened, less selfish towards the woman, than the paleolithic man? Is the woman less sacrificed, less enslaved, less dead spiritually in the one case than in the other?' [xiii] In fact Ulfheim and Maja offer each other more by demanding less than do Rubek and Irene.

Rubek promises Irene all the glory of the world and she swears to 'go with [him] to the world's end and to the end of life' and to 'serve him in all things' (369). Ulfheim merely suggests to Maja to 'try and draw the rags' of their tattered lives together and 'make some sort of a human life out of them' (442), asking her to go with him only 'as far and as long as [he] wants her' (445).

The contrast between celibate romanticism and realistic acknowledgement of sexuality is also found in the two-partite structure of 'Fugitives'. Harding's account of his bemused seduction of Lucy undermines the pathos of Rodney's story. When Harding comes across the girl wandering in London, he feeds her, tries to get her a place in the theatre, and finds her a place to stay. The seduction process (involving an attempt to get Lucy to pose for him) takes some time, during which two detectives are spotted at Harding's club. He panics — the girl is only seventeen; and a court case would destroy his reputation. He journeys to Ireland, where Lucy's parents welcome him as Galahad come to the rescue of their daughter. He travels back to London to tell Lucy that she is due to return to Ireland, where her marriage to a Chicago businessman has been arranged, and the two spend the night together (or at least this is what Harding implies). Harding's story makes Rodney realize an aspect of his past model that he has missed earlier: 'Lucy wanted life', Rodney says, 'and perhaps she will get her adventure sooner or later' (310). This desire for life, 'for the beautiful, miraculous earth life' is what Maja and Irene of *When We Dead Awaken* have in common with Lucy. [xiv]

Both Ibsen's play and Moore's story ask the question whether such awakening to life is possible, or whether, as Irene puts it, 'when we dead awaken … [w]e see that we have never lived' (431-2). However, while Ibsen is concerned with the ideal of the revival in general human terms, Moore's story examines this subject in the specifically Irish context.

There are several references in the story to the Irish Revival, in its different forms as the movement for the restoration of the Irish language, political independence, and cultural awakening. Rodney's friend Harding refers sceptically to his proposed 'wandering from cabin to cabin storing country idiom' (299) and Edward Martyn is mocked by both men for imagining the future Gaelic Ireland as a 'spring wood: burgeoning trees, nests in the branches, sculptors carving all day and perhaps all night in their studios … and painting of sea shores and forests' (298). Negative references to the movement for whose sake Moore returned to Ireland and wrote *The Untilled Field* are more numerous in the earlier version of the story. In 'In the Clay', as Rodney contemplates his imminent departure from Ireland, we are told that '[t]hey were talking about reviving the Gothic, but Rodney did not believe in their resurrections or in their renaissance or in their anything. "The Gael has had his day. The Gael is passing."' [xv] By using the word 'resurrection', Moore links his story of the destruction of the statue of the Virgin to the artist's inability, in Ibsen's play, to sculpt the allegorical representation of the Resurrection Day as a pure, unsullied woman.

This idealist dream of resurrection is impossible; people's small-mindedness and greed stand in its way. The statue in Ibsen's play, in Durbach's words, becomes 'a cancelled vision of Resurrection, [envisioning] the Land without Paradise and man's fallen state — mired in guilt and mortality.' [xvi]

And Moore's *Untilled Field* turned into a depiction of the land of failed possibilities, in which sexuality, conjugal happiness, and art are stunted by the inbred obeisance to dogma. Thus Rodney learns that his statue was not wrecked, as he first assumed, by a religious fanatic sent by the enraged priest but by 'two stupid little boys who have been taught their Catechism and will one day aspire to the priesthood' (297). In *Hail and Farewell* Moore speaks of his initial excitement about the Irish Revival as Ireland's long awaited awakening 'out of the great sleep of Catholicism.' [xvii] Here as well as in the earlier *Untilled Field*, he demonstrates how wrong he was to hope for this awakening. Catholicism, in its pernicious form, unique to Ireland, is set so deep that no resurrection is possible. In the words of Pat Connex, a character from 'The Wedding Feast' (the fifth story of The Untilled Field): 'We are a dead and alive lot' (100).

However, Moore's story of the destruction of a masterpiece is not merely a simplistic allegory of the demise of art in the Catholic climate of Ireland. 'In the Clay' contains a passage which in its resemblance to a line from *When We Dead Awaken* indicates the complexity of Moore's response to the problem of the artist's relation to his country. Rodney remembers telling Harding that

> he had given up the School of Art, that he was leaving Ireland, and Harding had thought that this was an extreme step, but Rodney had said that he did not want to die, that no one wanted to die less than he did, but he thought he would sooner die than go on teaching ... he was going ... to where there was art, to where there was the joy of life, out of a damp religious atmosphere in which nothing flourished but the religious vocation. [xviii]

The passage recalls Rubek's confession to Maja that he began to value life more than the hollow 'talk about the artist's vocation and the artist's mission':

> is not life in sunshine and in beauty a hundred times better worth while than to hang about to the end of your days in a raw, damp hole, and to wear yourself out in a perpetual struggle with lumps of clay and blocks of stone? (396)

The 'damp hole' of the artist's studio becomes in Moore's story the 'damp religious atmosphere' of Ireland. The implicit comparison to Ibsen's play suggests, however, that Rodney's choice of Italy over Ireland might be as hollow as Rubek's desire for the simple joys of life. Rubek eventually realizes that he is not 'at all adapted for seeking happiness in indolent enjoyment'; 'Life does not shape itself that way for me and those like me,' he tells his wife: 'I must go on working—producing one work after another—right up to my dying day' (398).

In 'The Way Back', Rodney's flight from Ireland is counterbalanced by Harding's proposed return there. His friends suggest that Harding's biographer 'will be puzzled to explain this … episode': 'You knew from the beginning that Paris was the source of all art … And having lived immersed in art till you're forty, you return to the Catholic Celt' (397). Rodney is unable to understand why Harding would wish to return to the country which is soon to be 'dead beyond hope of resurrection.' [xix] Harding's quest for the way back to Ireland is comparable to Rubek's decision in Ibsen's play to seek a reunion with Irene, his former model, who in her insanity believes that she has died because of Rubek's rejection of her. Both men return to their origins. Rubek takes Irene as his bride, in spite of her madness and her dubious past: 'Be who or what you please, for aught I care! For me you are the woman I see in my dreams of you' (453). And Harding is drawn to the newly discovered, pathetic, 'dear', 'wistful' and 'intimate' beauty of the country and its people. [xx] In Ibsen's play, the couple know that they face death as they ascend a mountain in a storm and are swept away by an avalanche. Such melodramatic devices are alien to Moore's vision, yet there is a hint of morbidity in Harding's comment in 'The Way Back' that 'No man wanders far from his grave sod.' [xxi] His return to Ireland, like Rubek's union-in-death with Irene, is an acceptance of mortality.

Ibsen's meditation on the contrast between the promise of immortality offered by art and its life-denying power allowed Moore to review his position within the Irish Literary Revival. 'Fugitives' demonstrates that the romantic ambitions of the Gaelic League and the Celtic Twilight are doomed to failure, not only because of the deep-set religious conservatism of the country. Idealistic revivalism—the creation of an Ireland of the imagination—is inherently flawed. Harding, who says, in 'The Way Back,' that he treasures what 'Paddy Durkin and Father Pat will say to [him] on the roadside' [xxii] far more than the discussions of the Italian renaissance, exemplifies a different approach to the Irish Revival. A true masterpiece of the movement would subject the country to realistic scrutiny. Accepting the country's prejudices and the dogmatic morbidity of its culture, such a masterpiece will not let any ideas of purity stand in the way of a truthful depiction of its men and women. Rubek in Ibsen's play became an acclaimed genius for a group statue of 'men and women as [he] knew them in real life' (416)—not for his original idea of the awakening of a pure unsullied woman. And Moore's realistic collection, as he claimed, was a landmark departure in Irish literature, not least for modifying the Celtic Twilight approach to the depiction of Ireland and anticipating Synge and Joyce. Yet, what Moore has in common with Ibsen is the knowledge that anti-idealist modernist art in spite of its promise of freedom may be as enslaving and deadening as the idealism that it has rejected.

At the end of *When We Dead Awaken* Rubek and Irene are killed in an avalanche, as they climb a mountain in the hope of a glorious life through death. Meanwhile Maja and Ulfheim take the dangerous route down the mountain. Maja sings triumphantly, rejoicing in her new freedom. But, as Durbach explains, 'there is fine irony in her confidence. No one on the *dodsens vei* [the deadly path, or the way towards death] is free. To move into the abyss of process, sexuality and change is to embrace death as surely as to transcend life in mythical constructs of the Romantic imagination.' xxiii

This realisation that salvation through anti-idealism is impossible is explored in Moore's stories in relation to Ireland's cultural revival. In the earlier narrative version of the story Harding may well believe that as an artist he is different from Rodney, that empathy with his countrymen and unabashed interest in their lives provide a way back to Ireland. Yet, 'Fugitives' implies that, just as Rodney and Harding's contrasting relationships with Lucy end with a similar inability to fulfil her desire for life, so may the two men's artistic engagements with Ireland prove to be opposite versions of failure. Consequently, in the final version Harding does not plan a return to Ireland. Nor does he give a lengthy explanation of this decision; he is only going for a few boring weeks collecting peasant idiom with Edward Martyn. In the final version, the way back is closed, the model has fled, and the participants of the Irish revival awaken in London to a realisation that Ireland has never let them live.

The interplay between *When We Dead Awaken* and Moore's three stories allows a glimpse of Moore as a reader. Ibsen's significance for Moore's theatrical activities is well established. Yet, Ibsen was more than that. In his fiction, Moore abstains from commenting on Ibsen's dramaturgy. Instead, he uses the image of the wild duck from Ibsen's play by that title to describe T. P. Gill (in *Salve*). xxiv In *Vale* he jokes that *Emperor and Galilean* would have been a better drama, had it contained a prophetic vision of the villainous workings of Catholicism in history. xxv *Master Builder* proved useful to Moore in his friendship with Hildegarde Hawthorne. In one of the sexually candid letters Moore wrote to Hawthorne he alluded to Hilda, a young woman who worships the older Solness for his talent.[xxvi] And fourteen years earlier, Moore recalled *Master Builder* and Aline's grief over her burnt-out house and her lost childhood treasures when writing of his own familial seat. [xxvii] Not unlike Joyce's Dedalus, who is said to feel the spirit of Ibsen going like a keen wind outside Baird Stone Cutting Works in Talbot street, [xxviii] Moore made Ibsen part of his vision of Ireland—his plays are transformed and mocked by the Irish realities but still glimpsed at in the most unsuspected places.

NOTES

[i]   James Joyce, 'The Day of the Rabblement' (1901) in *James Joyce, Occasional, Critical and Political Writing*, ed. Kevin Barry (Oxford University Press, 2000) p.52.

[ii]   Joyce's review of *When We Dead Awaken* entitled 'Ibsen's New Drama' was published in *The Fortnightly Review* in April 1900. See Occasional, Critical and Political Writing, pp. 30-49.

[iii] Yeats's speech on the subject was reported in 'Dramatic Ideals and the Irish Literary Theatre,' *Freeman's Journal* (6 May 1899), 5. See also *Beltaine: The Organ of the Irish Literary Theatre* (May 1899-April 1900), repr. in one volume (London: Frank Cass, 1970), 6.

[iv]   George Moore, *The Untilled Field* (London: William Heinemann, 1931), 304. Further references to this edition will be cited parenthetically in the text.

[v]   The assonance of Rubek's name with Rodin's was noted by G. B. Shaw in *The Quintessence of Ibsenism: Now Completed to the Death of Ibsen* (London: Constable and Company, 1922), 150.

[vi]   George Moore, *The Untilled Field* (London: Fisher Unwin, 1903), 25.

[vii] Henrik Ibsen, *When We Dead Awaken, The Collected Works of Henrik Ibsen*, ed. William Archer, 11 vols. (New York: Charles Scribner's Sons, 1908-10), XI, 415-7, hereafter cited parenthetically in the text.

[viii] Errol Durbach, *'Ibsen the Romantic': Analogues of Paradise in Later Plays* (Athens, Georgia: The University of Georgia Press, 1982), 141.

[ix]   George Moore, [*Vale*], *Hail and Farewell*, ed. Richard Cave (Gerrards Cross: Colin Smythe, 1976), 609.

[x]   Durbach, *Ibsen the Romantic*, 142.

[xi]   Moore, [*Salve*], *Hail and Farewell*, 269.

[xii] Shaw, *Quintessence*, 149.

[xiii] Ibid. 149

xiv   Both women accuse Rubek of denying them the opportunity to experience life fully. Maja decides to leave Rubek in search of adventure and to 'let life take place of all the rest', describing their marriage as living in a 'clammy cage' without 'sunlight or fresh air, but only gilding and great petrified ghosts of people all round the walls' (442); Irene refers to her mental disorder or nervous breakdown as something 'that always happen[s] when a young warm-blooded woman dies' (367).

xv   Moore, *The Untilled Field*, 1903 edition, 6.

xvi   Durbach, *Ibsen the Romantic*, 139.

xvii   Moore, [*Ave*], *Hail and Farewell*, 56.

xviii   Moore, *The Untilled Field*, 1903 edition, 6.

xix   This comment by Rodney appears in the 1903 American (Philadelphia: Lippincott) edition of *The Untilled Field* (378), but not in the 1903 Fisher Unwin edition.

xx   Moore, *The Untilled Field*, 1903 American edition, 419. The sentence from which these terms are taken reads '… I perceived a pathetic beauty in the country itself that I had not perceived before; and a year afterwards I was driving about the Dublin mountains, and met two women on the road; there was something pathetic and wistful about them, something intimate and I felt drawn towards them'.

xxi   Ibid.

xxii   Ibid, 420.

xxiii   Durbach, *Ibsen the Romantic*, 147. Moore, [*Salve*], *Hail and Farewell*, 310.
Moore, [*Salve*], *Hail and Farewell*, 356-7.
Moore to Hildegarde Hawthorne 30 March 1910, *George Moore on Parnassus* Letters (1900-1933) to *Secretaries, Publishers, Printers, Agents, Literati, Friends, and Acquaintance*s, ed. Helmut E. Gerber (Newark: University of Delaware Press, 1988), 178-9.
Moore, Conversations in Ebury Street. (New York: Boni and Liveright, 1924), 314-5.
James Joyce, *A Portrait of the Artist as a Young Man*. Eds. Hans Walter Gabler and Walter Hettche (New York and London: Garland, 1993), p. 203.

xxiv   Moore, [*Salve*], *Hail and Farewell*, 310.

xxv   Moore, [*Salve*], *Hail and Farewell*, 356-7.

xxvi   Moore to Hildegarde Hawthorne 30 March 1910, *George Moore on Parnassus: Letters* (1900-1933) to *Secretaries, Publishers, Printers, Agents, Literati, Friends, and Acquaintances*, ed. Helmut E. Gerber (Newark: University of Delaware Press, 1988), 178-9.

xxvii   Moore, *Conversations in Ebury Street*. (New York: Boni and Liveright, 1924), 314-5.

xxviii   James Joyce, *A Portrait of the Artist as a Young Man*. Eds. Hans Walter Gabler and Walter Hettche (New York and London: Garland, 1993), p. 20.

Louis de Paor

BÁISTEACH

An cumhrán a chaitheadh sí sna déaga
is ailceimic a colainne tríd,
farraige, féar is fiúise
i naoi déag seachtó a naoi,
do shiúl thar bráid
sa tsráid aréir
nóscumaliom mar bháisteach,
comhartha broinne ar a rúitín clé
is lúba airgid ar a riostaí geanmnaí.

Mar a bheadh scáth fearthainne sa ghaoth
d'iompaigh mo chroí
isteach is amach
faoin gcith cumhra
ná fliuchfadh barra mo mhéar.

Nuair a d'éirigh an ghrian
thar mhaol gualainne aniar,
bhí cumhracht cnis
ar bhláthanna teochreasa
ag briseadh
tré leacacha na cathrach.

RAIN

That perfume she wore in her teens
shot through
with the alchemy of her body
—sea, grass and fuchsia
in nineteen seventy nine—
walked past on the street last night
as couldn't-care-less as rain,
a birthmark on her left ankle
and silver bracelets on her untouchable wrists.

Like an umbrella in a gale,
my heart turned
inside out
under a drench of fragrance
that left my fingertips
bone-dry.

When the sun rose
over her shoulder,
tropical flowers
perfumed like skin
burst through paving stones
all over the city.

Louis de Paor

IDIR DHÁ LINN

Tá am na gcuairteoirí thart

is táim im sheasamh ag stad
an bhus, trasna na sráide
ó Oispidéal Ríoga na mBan,

greim docht agam
ar lámha na leanaí.

Tá Áthas ag cur di
in ard a cinn, mar is gnáth,

agus Amhras, a deartháir,
ag pléascadh le huisce.

Ainneoinn na dtreoracha
a thugais dom ar ball
níl a fhios agam
ó thalamh an domhain

cén fhuinneog
a bhfuileann tú
id sheasamh
led bhurla beag
dóchais is caca.

Níl eadrainn ach
leithead Sráid Grattan,
ceithre urlár

agus pasáiste gearr
antaiseipteach

ach tá sé ródhéanach
cheana le dul siar

thar na poill bheaga
i ndromchla an ama,

mo dhá láimh
a chur timpeall ort
is féachaint
thar do ghualainn amach

ar an gcréatúr bocht
ag stad an bhus

a bhfuil aoibh
an tsonais ar a bhéal,
agus greim scaoilte
ag na leanaí
ar a lámha.

Tá Inné ag cur di
gan stop, Inniu
ag pléascadh le huisce,

Amárach ina codladh,
caoch ar ucht a máthar.

Louis de Paor

IN THE MEANTIME

Visiting time is over.

And I'm standing at the bus stop,
across the street from
the Royal Women's Hospital,

holding the children's hands
as tight as I can.

Happiness is prattling away
non-stop as usual,

while Not-so-sure, her brother,
is bursting for a piss.

After all the directions
you gave me a short while ago

I can't for the life of me remember
which window you're at

with your little bundle
of hope and shit.

There's nothing between us,
only the width of Grattan Street,

four floors and a short
antiseptic corridor

but it's already too late
to cross over

the small potholes
in the surface of time,

to put my arms around you
and look out over your shoulder

at the poor fool
standing there at the bus stop

smiling happily,
with his children holding

his hands — Yesterday
talking non-stop,

Today bursting for a piss,

Tomorrow, blind, asleep
in her mother's arms.

Áine Tierney

MY GRANDMOTHER AND THE RUNT

My Grandmother threatened us with her death for many years—you'll miss me when I'm gone; you'll be sorry when I'm dead. She went on a yearly pilgrimage to Knock, always taking me with her, and each time she declared the visit to be her last. She would cry on her return, telling me she would never see Knock again, because she would be dead, and I'd feel an itch of crossness spread across my skin that she could say such things. To annoy her, I'd tell her that death was hardly imminent for a woman who ate three breakfasts a day and that I had no doubt she'd see ninety—that, I could be sure, would sting.

She died of cancer in her eighty-ninth year. For a long time, her death was all of her life that I could contemplate. It reduced her life to the swish of tracksuit bottoms in hospital corridors; the smell of red medicated soap; the angry mass of her tumour. On the 10th of July, 2001, on the stroke of 6 o'clock as the Angelus rang out; she died. She was buried on my twenty second birthday, two days later.

Now I remember a short woman, only five foot, with a fat belly and arms too long for her body, weighted down with clenched fists that she swung like pendulums when she walked, as if to keep herself balanced. She was an evangelist, set to save the souls of those around her. "Jesus, Jesus, Jesus," she would whisper under her breath. She would teach us, my brother and I, prayers of different potency. "Jesus, Mary and Joseph, save souls": that was enough to swing open the gates of heaven to let through one poor sinner from purgatory; there were special, longer incantations for group passes.

She had brown eyes that sparkled with devilment, but looked black when she was cross. Children gave her great pleasure, for she loved fighting with them. Myself and my brother kept her going, scolding us for getting our clothes muddy, not keeping our rooms tidy. But this was all mild stuff, just to stop her powder going damp. Her shining role was as our defender. Liam Ryan, our neighbour across the road, was in the same class in school as my brother and myself and there would be the odd childish row between us. If

Nanny got any whiff of these rows, no matter who was actually in the right or wrong, she'd be down the road to Ryan's wall, barely hitting the ground, and calling for him to, "come out and face her." She would get no thanks from us for her involvement, and there was nearly always another row at home after the warrior returned. This would probably end with me slamming the door, leaving her behind it, but her voice would follow me—"look off at her in a temper, with the straight back and the crooked nose."

She also had a great love of poetry, often reciting verses out loud. She could remember all the poetry she learned in school; Wordsworth's *Daffodils* and Padraic Pearce's *The Wayfarer* would often be recited with great feeling. It was this romantic streak and love of poetry—both of which she passed onto me—that got me into the following spot of bother.

When I was thirteen and started secondary school, I developed a major crush on one of the older boys. His greatest feature in my eyes was his height. He was about four and a half foot, far less intimidating than the other lads. The first time I saw him he was being pulled out of a bin, no doubt after being dumped there first. They used to bundle him about the place and call him "the runt," which would raise my ardour to even higher levels.

I was a bookish child, and I think that all bookish girls are tomboys at heart. You have all these male heroes to identify with, princes after damsels in distress. The story may be called sleeping beauty, but who cares for her dreams? It is the prince that sees all the action and who we follow. I wanted to be the hero, not the rescued. It was therefore only natural that I would choose to do swimming, as he did, for PE, and that my time in the pool would be spent casting eyes in his direction. Now, you may think that this was to catch a glimpse of his naked torso, but such things were beneath my notice, rather, I lived for the day that I would see his head bobbing in and out of the water—just drowning ever so slightly—so I could swim over, get him in an arm lock, and bring him to safety. Generally, I didn't believe in throwing my affections away on those that didn't need them. I remember being told his mother had passed away. This snippet of information was quickly transmuted in my mind to her dying in childbirth—having just given birth to the runt. I could picture the poor baby, red, raw and undersized, being handed to a cold and heartbroken father, incapable of loving anyone ever again—especially not the runt. And the day I found out he had a step-mother—I knew he was my ideal man.

I would peek at him from behind corners, one glimpse of him could inspire a dozen soppy verses. Valentine's day was coming and I wrote a card, and stuffed it with A4 pages upon A4 pages of my heartfelt, teenage love poetry. Though I had absolutely no intention of ever sending it to him, no detail was to be left undone, so I put his address on the envelope. My young self saw my affections as a beautiful, painful unrequited love and I couldn't have had it any other way. If he had approached me, I'd have been overcome and most likely would have run in the other direction.

Valentine's day came and to get myself in the mood I went to read my verses and spray them with a little of my Grandmother's perfume. Gone. Disappeared. Such things were normally hidden down my doll Blondie's knickers where I thought they would be safe, but somebody had gone a rummaging. War rose. It quickly became apparent that my Grandmother had been over- taken by a wave of romance and decided to try and play cupid by sending the card. She had plucked the card, filled with romantic verses, from down the back of Blondie's knickers, put a stamp on it, and dropped it into a letter box.

All I could feel was wild panic—I would have to leave the school, no, the country. How could I face him again, and he knowing the thoughts I'd had about his lips as soft as cushions. My Grandmother was completely relaxed and logical about it, well if he knows you like him he might respond, and sure if he doesn't there wasn't anything bad in it anyway. Such reasoning went well over my head. I still cannot think of that incident without cringing, of him waking up on Valentine's morning, being almost knocked over by the smell of perfume, reading about his doe-like eyes and hair that waved like the wind through fields of corn.

It is hard for me to believe that it is over ten years since she died, it doesn't feel that long. She failed in making me a good housekeeper, she always complained I was a streal, yet all her efforts have made no difference—I'm still untidy. But I learnt so much from her too. She taught me how to bake apple tarts, make jam, showed me what kindness was, and I'm afraid she passed on her fiery side to me as well. Also, though it may not have been her intention, she taught me never to go rummaging in the knickers of anybody else's doll.

Kevin Higgins

THE NECESSARY ARRANGEMENTS

Write it all down, she says, on the back
of a Tax Clearance Cert, or one
of those dead political manifestos
that keep you up all night in the study:

what you want done
when you step out in front
of a terminal 46 bus, or
get your leg caught in a passing
combine harvester; cease to be
anywhere you can give the world
the benefit of your advice.

She says, last time she looked,
most of my parts were in adequate
working order. But it's never too
early to start choosing
a hat for the funeral.

No hat, I tell her, turn up
with a black scarf fastened
to your grief stricken head. If at all possible
get someone to sponsor the coffin
and every cent you can
from the relatives. Put
my dentures and other
detachable bits immediately
up for auction. Employ

a church load of Anglicans
to tell lovely lies about what I was like;
a choir to sing *Holidays In Cambodia*
as I'm rolled out the door. Poets
who shuffle up sheepish
demanding a microphone
from which to sing my praises
should be buried with me
and never spoken of again.

If the city fathers
name anything after me,
make sure it's a block of flats
with Thatcherite hallways
where skinny dogs can disagree
to their hearts' discontent,
and sellers of socialist newspapers
not yet born
can tell children with cigarettes
and guys in boxer shorts they got
free with *The News of The World*
about the working class and how
they have nothing to lose
but their tracksuit bottoms.

Apart from that, do
whatever you think appropriate.

Trish Finnan

ONION

Onion
peeling thin
translucent
paper skin
bulb of light
pungent pickled pearls
concentric silken shifts
ivory shells
spherical symbol of the universe
for the ancients
onion *unus* one
slice
slivers
stings
tears
drop.

Mike McCormack

from: PILGRIM X

I must have slept into the early afternoon, three hours at least. When I stood out, the light had that grey, sifted look which settles in with the dusk. I stood in the doorway of the hut stretching the stiffness out of my bones, my back and sides. The pain in my shoulder was somewhat dulled but my arm could not straighten to its full extension. So I stood there in the grey light rotating my shoulder, watching a pale moon labouring up into the sky. A van pulled into the common area and blasted its horn, two long blasts. The sound drew men and women from the adjoining huts. Index appeared beside me.

"Knacks," she said breezily, "come on, this'll be good."

She drew me by the hand into the small crowd which had gathered around the van, a vehicle I recognised as a miraculous composite of disparate parts and good faith. With no matching panels anywhere it gave the impression it might collapse at any moment in a heap. What had once been a Toyota HiAce now had its rear end extended to accommodate a flat bed on which stood a large drum secured with brackets and chains to the chassis. The door swung open and a short, barrel shaped man stepped out. He spent a moment pushing the tail of his shirt into the back of his trousers, gazing around at the gathering crowd till his eyes finally lit on Frank.

"If a man was looking for forty gallons of diesel would he be standing in the right place?" he called loudly.

"He might," Frank said cagily, "but any man looking for forty gallons of diesel is asking for a lot."

"Forty gallons," the knack persisted, "red or green, this man wouldn't be choosy."

"He mightn't be choosy but forty gallons wouldn't come cheap no matter what colour it was."

"He might have to bulk the deal out with copper piping or lead flashing—how would that go down."

"If a rate of exchange could be fixed a deal could be struck."

"But suppose the man had neither lead nor copper."

"Then he'd be wasting his time and my time."

"And that wouldn't be good, as the man said."

"No, that would not be good."

"Suppose this man had certain skills—would they be considered legal tender?"

"We're still talking about the same man?"

"One and the same, or a close relative of the same."

"We could always talk."

"Talk is cheap. But it won't put a basin of stir-about in a man's hand or milk in his wains' belly."

"Any talk here is underwrit in good faith. The gate is there; you can take it or leave it."

The knack leaned back against the truck. After a moment he nodded and raised his left hand.

"Mayofosam," he said.

Frank raised his hand in return, "Mayofosam."

It was clear from the easing of the atmosphere that some sort of understanding or truce had been established after the formal opening exchanges. Now the two men took a step towards each other and stood in the centre of the space.

"It's been a while, Frankie boy," the knack said.

"The years don't be long passing."

"Where do they all go?"

The knack now looked at the crowd with open curiosity, sometimes nodding in recognition or holding for a moment on the faces of the younger ones. His gaze lingered a long time on my own before passing to Index.

"A lot of new faces Frank, young and old. They're not all yours, are they?"

"No, I've my hands full as it is."

"You haven't tied a knot in it yet have you? A man like you would be fond of the wren's nest."

"It's a sign of growth, I'm told."

The knack grinned and took a few steps away from the truck. It took me a moment to realise he was heading towards me.

"This man here, Frank, does he have a name?"

"None that I know of, or if he has he's keeping it to himself."

"Another Xman?"

"Yes."

His face opened in a wide smile as he held out his hand. "Jimmy the Knack," he said, "and you're…?"

And that's as simple as it was. I leaned forward to shake his hand and as I did so the right side of my head exploded.

I saw the move clearly in retrospect and to some extent admired it. Taking his hand would have turned my body towards him, leaving the whole of my right side open. And he would have drawn it up from his hip to where it detonated over my cheekbone. And whether I fell forward or backwards I will never know but either way it was curtains; it was a simple move but brutally effective.

A left uppercut.

He would tell me later that he called it The Mary Ann.

Once again I woke in pain only this time it had two new focal points. The pain in the side of my face which consumed my whole head was offset and balanced by a deep burning pain lower down in the back of my left leg and it was as if my whole being was strung between these two flames. It took me a long and tough effort of will to separate myself from them but eventually I was aware that Frank had his arm around me and was hauling me up into a sitting position. Now the room around me swirled, all its walls and surfaces interleaved and began to slip below a surface which threatened to close in over itself… Then I was spluttering and choking; ice-cold water snagged in my throat and shot out through my nose. Through a squall of spluttering and coughing I saw Index somewhere beyond my feet, gazing up at me without expression. To her back, standing against the wall the knack was using a strip of cloth to clean a terrible looking blade which looked like it might have been used for skinning dogs.

"More," Frank urged, pushing an enamel cup against my mouth, "drink more."

The ice water cut through the fog of pain and confusion and I realised that I was lying on the table of the longhouse. I had many questions but when I opened my mouth to speak the effort pushed me below the horizon of consciousness once more.

Frank's was the only face which swam into focus when I woke the second time. He was sitting with his eyes closed and his arms crossed on his chest as if he had been there for some time. When I tried to shift myself off the table he rose up.

"Slowly," he said, "take it easy."

He put a hand between my shoulder blades and levered me up into a sitting position. After a few swaying seconds the room eventually righted itself, resolving through a glare of fevered pain. Now that my vision had cleared I was aware that myself and Frank were the only two in the long house – there was no sign of the knack or Index. Whatever about the knack the room seemed incomplete without her; even my own condition seemed incomplete without her. Frank tipped my head back and I choked down a couple of mouthfuls of water before pushing him away.

My whole being was now drawn towards the wound in my calf muscle. It was heavily bandaged and pulsed with fierce heat and pain. I noticed also that my wrist was wrapped all around with grey electrician's tape. Focusing on what I thought was another wound I felt instead a kind of fevered insectile vibrating beneath the tape.

"Don't touch that," Frank warned sharply, "that's the trace. Leave it alone and it will be ok there for a day or two. Don't start poking at it. We will have to offload it as soon as we can so we're taking a trip as soon as you're fit."

The vicious buzzing of whatever it was that lay under the tape hummed along the length of my arm and the thought of having to endure this sensation for the next day or so sickened me. What the hell was it? Where had it come from? Frank sat down beside the table and handed me the cup of water again.

"That's the trace or the beacon that was implanted in you when you were sentenced here. No one in here knows for sure what they transmit or to whom they transmit but we are fairly sure that they are more than a GPS beacon. From what we know they appear to be driven by the movement of our bodies, rather like those antique kinematic watches. So that's why it's taped to your hand. It will be fooled into transmitting real telemetry for the time being but after about a day and a half it will begin to deteriorate because it is trapped under that tape—we now know that these things need the free run of your body or they begin to deteriorate."

"The free run of my body?"

"Yes, this trace is specific to you, it has the run of your body so that it transmits your GPS reference and other information about your organism. We are certain of the first part of that but we only speculate on the second part—we have no way of verifying what it is these biobots transmit. But yes, it needs the full scope of your body; imagine a bluebottle in a forty gallon barrel, something like that."

"And the knack…what does he…?"

"Jimmy removed it. Taking those things out is a real skill, it takes a lot of time and patience; you would have admired it if you had seen it," he said cheerfully.

"That knife?"

"Yes."

"And you trust him," I blurted in sudden rage, "with that fucking knife and…"

"…and if I was you I'd be grateful to the big man. Take a look—he left you with a single wound. I've seen some men cut to ribbons from having these things removed. But not many have Jimmy's patience; he took his time with it, fair play to him. Three days he followed it, just standing there attuning himself to it and when he finally pounced he got it first time. I've never seen it done so accurately, not with a single strike anyway."

"Three days?"

"Yes, three days, no sleep or eating, Jimmy just standing there tracing you up and down with the tip of the blade, waiting for his moment."

"How long have I been out?"

"A couple of more hours and you would have been starting your fifth day. I was beginning to get worried." He got up and turned his chair into the table. Putting his arm under my ribs he levered me off the table and we made our way towards the door. "Get as much sleep as you can tonight, we're going on a trip tomorrow."

Eva Bourke

SONG

for Adrian, Cliodhna, Clea and Lesy

The children played in a narrow back garden
without end. Behind the rough stone wall
the town began, full of its own consequence,
covering a small part of the earth

with solemn buildings, canals and streets.
Seagulls stood watch above the garden
balanced on up-draughts, and a septet
of sharp-eyed geese passed overhead

in a music of strong white wings.
The green boat of the garden had long
grown roots into the ground and lay
dreaming of ocean forests, of ferrying

the children through fields of water.
At times the days were short. Then the windows
in the house peered out into the rain
full of a curious orange glow

but in June nights the elder trees lit their dim lanterns
and the blackbird sang until late its sweet
unending variations. They played with twigs,
snails, a blue-veined stone.

The twigs promised a star, the snails
promised a journey, the stone promised
a half-moon, a new sister, a handful of red berries,
a circus tent, a nest with five nestlings,

an apple tree beneath which a pair
of small capable watchdogs were asleep,
a book whose covers were green
as the boat in the grass, green

as the windfall apples, the poplars beyond
the canal. As the evening light faded
we watched them rewrite on its pages
the chapters of beginning in a language we had lost.

A bird raised its piccolo to play a tune,
a cloud looked down and sailed past.

Eva Bourke

RENVYLE

It wasn't that this patchwork of low-lying fields, reeds,
brambles and boreens lay radiant
in the August sun, and that in the one-street
village of Tully, I noticed that the Sunday painter,

in true naïve realist style, had installed
a fiberglass steed on the pub roof, black, life-size,
perhaps a symbol—what of was anyone's guess—
then primed the houses in the long terrace

according to a blatant fairground colour scheme
and, devoting meticulous attention to each detail,
placed miniature gardens by the doors and on the sills
nor was it that the sea in the near foreground to my right

went through an age-old routine of hide and seek,
first made a marimba music with the pebbles on the strand,
rolling them up and down and up and back again
at an infinitesimal and indefinite pitch of drawn-

out tiny clatters, rattles, clinks, withdrew then, yawned and bid
its time for the return, then slowly rose as though its heart's
desire were to sweep across all thresholds in the world,
its energy refreshed by the long ebb-tide wait,

rose up and blazed its blue advance path open wide,
nor was it the blackberry vines that dripped with fruit,
basalt beads dropping at a touch into tall grass
while the wind ran its rake through wayside

meadowsweet and fuchsia bush, nor that from a gate
of grey light and lark twitter stepped a mare
and her two months-old lanky foal,
slowly as if they stepped out of a marvellous tale,

spot-lit beneath the driving clouds then strode
towards me to get a better look but held
back by a barrier of brambles, rampant like long rolls
of barbed wire, they lost interest, turning to each other

as if they were the sole beings alive in all of Tully
deserving of attention, and so they were, this morning
as they sauntered, manes and tails wind-tousled,
across the blackberry field, their muscles

moving in unison at a dancing pace, the foal nestled
close, performed a *double à droite* and nuzzled
beneath her warm round flank for milk, nor the white
circlet round his delicate hind fetlock on the right,

nor that the neighbouring houses paid little heed and held
to the timetable of the punctual yellow bus
trundling unmusically along the narrow hilly roads
full of school children and books, each printed line a truth

which the bus followed as a reader's finger might
follow a line of text, nor that irises lifted their heads
up in the hedge to get a glimpse of me as I entered
a tunnel whose one wall was golden and the other red,

but that I saw down by the pier my brother stand beside the boat-
wreck through whose broken ribs colt's foot and bind-
weed grew, saw him turn and walk away and was heart-
sick in a wide open room with ceilings of wind.

Dillon Johnston

LAST COURSE

for Adrian & Cliodhna, lovers of apples

I'd like to be the apple of your eye,
perhaps not yours alone but also those
of many eyes, the blushing object of
a groundswell of rooting, the crushing press
of fans at my stage door or else the squeeze
at the stage apron, signing autographs.
I'd feel the bake of warm adoration
in response to my tart repartee. Now,
at last I'll receive my just deserts, or
else sweet dreams curdling, stewed, and soured,
apt applause softening to applesauce,
just mush from what is overmuch desired.

Biographical Notes

GUINN BATTEN teaches at Washington University in St. Louis, where she lives with her husband Dillon Johnston. The author of *The Orphaned Imagination: Melancholy and Commodity Culture in English Romanticism* and an editor of *Romantic Generations: Essays in Honor of Robert F. Gleckner*, she co-edited with Dillon Johnston "Irish Poetry in English, 1940-2000" for *The Cambridge History of Irish Literature*. She has published over a dozen essays on contemporary Irish poetry, managed until 1990 the Wake Forest University Press's Irish Poetry Series, and is currently writing a book on Irish poetry of the Troubles and the Romantic Enlightenment.

EOIN BOURKE is Professor Emeritus of German at NUI Galway. He specialized in several research areas including "Vormärz", intercultural studies, travel and expedition literature, the critical "Volksstück", literature as testimony. His book *Poor green Erin,* presenting German travel-writers on Ireland from before the 1798 rebellion to after the Great Famine, appeared in 2011 to great acclaim.

EVA BOURKE was born in Germany. She has published six collections of poetry, most recently *Piano* (Dedalus Press 2011) and has edited *Landing Places* (with Borbála Faragó), an anthology of immigrant poets in Ireland, (Dedalus 2010), and several anthologies and collections of German and Irish poets in translation. Her collections *The Latitude of Naples* and *piano* have appeared in Italian translation. (Kolibris Edizioni, Bologna). She has taught poetry at the Joiner Centre at the University of Massachusetts and presently teaches in the M.A. in Writing Program at NUI, Galway. She is a member of Aosdána.

EDWARD BOYNE is a poet and fiction writer based in Galway. Twice shortlisted for the Hennessy Award and the Francis McManus award, his work has been published in a variety of journals including *Cyphers*, *The SHOp* and the *Cúirt Annual*. His collection of poems *The Day of the Three Swans* was published in 2010.

KEN BRUEN has been a finalist for the Edgar, Barry, and Dagger Awards. The Private Eye Writers of America presented him with the Shamus Award for the Best Novel of 2003 for *The Guards*, the book that introduced Jack Taylor. In 2010, the Mystery Readers International bestowed the Macavity Award on Ken and Reed Farrel Coleman for their crime novel *Tower*. Ken lives in Galway, Ireland.

MEGAN BUCKLEY completed her PhD at the Department of English at NUI, Galway in 2012. She is the author of a number of articles on contemporary poetry by Irish women and on the history of Irish publishing.

SANDRA BUNTING is presently working on a new poetry collection and, along with other contributors, is a coauthor of *The Claddagh: Stories from the Water's Edge* (History Press, 2013). Her first collection of poems, *Identified in Trees*, was published by Marram Press. She holds an M.A. in Writing from NUI, Galway, and is the recent winner of a Prairie Schooner Glenna Luschei award for poetry. She lives in Montréal.

PATRICIA BYRNE is a County Mayo native who currently lives in Limerick. For almost three decades she worked in regional economic development with the government agency Shannon Development. She completed an M.A. in Writing at NUI, Galway during 2007/2008, where she took a course convened by Adrian Frazier in creative nonfiction. Her book, *The Veiled Woman of Achill*, recently published by the Collins Press, grew from work she commenced during the M.A. programme. The book was launched in May 2012 during the Heinrich Böll Memorial Weekend.

LAURA ANN CAFFREY holds a B.A. in English and German and is a recent graduate of the M.A. in Writing programme at NUIG. Her poems have been published in *The Stinging Fly*, *Crannóg* and *ROPES*.

MOYA CANNON was born in Donegal. She has published four collections of poetry, her most recent being *Hands* (Carcanet, 2011). She has been editor of *Poetry Ireland Review*, and is a member of Aosdána.

LOUIS DE PAOR has been involved with the contemporary renaissance of poetry in Irish since 1980 when he was first published in the poetry journal *Innti* which he subsequently edited for a time. A four-time winner of the Oireachtas prize for the best collection of poems in Irish, he lived in Australia from 1987 to 1996. A bilingual collection *Ag greadadh bas sa reilig/Clapping in the cemetery* was published by Cló Iar-Chonnachta in November 2005. A second bilingual volume *agus rud eile de/and another thing* (2010) includes artwork by Kathleen Furey and a recording of poems with musical settings by Ronan Browne. His *Selected Poems* have just been published by Coiscéim.

THEO DORGAN is a poet, prose writer, translator and editor. Among his recent books are *Sailing for Home* and *Time on the Ocean*, accounts of two deep-sea voyages under sail. His most recent collection of poems, *Greek*, was published by Dedalus Press, which will also publish a new collection by him in 2013. His first novel, *Making Way*, was published by New Island in March 2013. Dorgan is a member of Aosdána.

NOEL DUFFY's collection of two novellas, *The Return Journey & Our Friends Electric*, was published in early 2011 by Ward Wood Publishing (London). His debut poetry collection, *In the Library of Lost Objects*, was also published by Ward Wood in summer 2011. It was been shortlisted for the Eithne and Rupert Strong Award for the best debut collection by an Irish author. He was a recipient of an Arts Council of Ireland Bursary for Literature in 2012. Duffy holds an M.A. in Writing from NUI, Galway.

SUSAN MILLAR DuMARS has published three poetry collections with Salmon Poetry, *Big Pink Umbrella* (2008), *Dreams for Breakfast* (2010) and *The God Thing* (2013) and one book of short stories, *Lights in the Distance*, with Doire Press in 2010. Her work has appeared in publications in the US and Europe and in several anthologies, including *The Best of Irish Poetry 2010*. She has read from her work in the US, Europe and Australia. She lives in Galway, where she and her husband coordinate the Over the Edge readings series.

TRISH FINNAN is originally from Edgeworthstown in County Longford and now lives in Galway. She works as a librarian at NUI, Galway and has recently completed an M.A. in Writing at NUI, Galway.

NDREK GJINI is an Albanian journalist and writer. He is the author of many books, including a collection of poetry in English. He holds BA and BA Honours in Heritage Studies from the Galway Mayo Institute of Technology, Galway, Ireland, BA and H.Dip in Education from the University of Shkoder, Albania, and MA in Writing, from the National University of Ireland, Galway, Ireland. He worked for some time for the Galway Arts Office and is the editor of the recently published *Galway Review*.

MICHAEL GORMAN was born in Sligo. His last collection of poetry was *Up She Flew* (Salmon, 1992). He has taught poetry for many years in international MFA programmes and in the M.A. in Writing at NUI, Galway.

EAMON GRENNAN is from Dublin, and taught for many years at Vassar College, and currently teaches in the graduate writing program of Columbia University. His most recent collections are *Out of Sight: New & Selected Poems* (Graywolf, USA), and *But the Body* (Gallery, Ireland). He has translated the poems of Leopardi (Dedalus and Princeton), and co-translated (with Rachel Kitzinger) *Oedipus at Colonus* (Oxford). He lives in Poughkeepsie and in Connemara.

GERARD HANBERRY is a prizewinning poet and writer who has published three collections of poetry: *Rough Night* (2002), *Something Like Lovers* (2005), and At *Grattan Road* (Salmon Poetry, 2009), as well as a biography of Oscar Wilde and his family entitled *More Lives Than One: The Remarkable Wilde Family Through the*

Generations (The Collins Press, 2011). A fourth collection of poetry, *What Our Shoes Say About Us*, will be published by Salmon in 2013. A teacher of English at St. Enda's College, Galway, he also delivers various courses on writing and writers. Gerard Hanberry holds an M.A. in Writing from NUI, Galway.

JAMES HARPUR has published five books of poetry with Anvil Press, including *Angels and Harvesters* (2012), a Poetry Book Society Recommendation, and *The Dark Age* (2007), which won the Michael Hartnett Award. He has also published *Fortune's Prisoner* (2007), the poems of Boethius, and *Love Burning in the Soul*, an introduction to the Christian mystics. He lives in West Cork.

AIDEEN HENRY writes short fiction, poetry and drama. Her short story, "Saibh," was shortlisted for the Francis McManus Award in 2011. Her story, "Idling," was shortlisted for the same award in 2012. Her first collection of short stories, *Hugging Thistles*, was published with Arlen House in April 2013. Her first poetry collection, *Hands Moving at the Speed of Falling Snow*, was published by Salmon Poetry in 2010, when she was shortlisted for the Emerging Poetry Section of the Hennessy XO Literary Awards. She is currently working on her second poetry collection.

KEVIN HIGGINS facilitates poetry workshops at Galway Arts Centre, teaches creative writing at Galway Technical Institute, and is on the Brothers of Charity Away With Words programme. He is Writer-in-Residence at Merlin Park Hospital, and is the poetry critic for the *Galway Advertiser*. He has published three collections of poems: The Boy With No Face (2005), *Time Gentlemen, Please* (2008) and *Frightening New Furniture* (2010) with Salmon Poetry. *Mentioning The War*, a collection of his essays and reviews, was published by Salmon in April 2012. Kevin's fourth collection of poetry, *The Ghost In The Lobby*, will appear from Salmon in Spring 2013.

RITA ANN HIGGINS is an internationally acclaimed poet and writer and a native of Galway. She has published ten collections of poetry, her most recent being *Ireland is Changing Mother* (Bloodaxe 2011). A memoir in prose and poetry, *Hurting God*, was published by Salmon in 2010. She is the author of six stage plays and one screenplay. She has been awarded numerous prizes and awards, among others an honorary professorship. She is a member of Aosdána.

Founding and now advising editor of the Wake Forest University Press, which is the United States's major publisher of Irish poetry, DILLON JOHNSTON has written essays and books on Irish and British poetry.

HUGO KELLY has won many writing awards for his short stories in Ireland and the UK, and has twice been shortlisted for the Hennessy Award for Emerging Fiction. His work has appeared in various publications including the *Sunday Tribune*, various Fish Short

Story Anthologies, *The Stinging Fly*, and *Verbal Magazine* amongst others. RTÉ Radio 1 and BBC Radio 4 have broadcast his short stories. Hugo lives and works in Galway.

THOMAS KILROY is a playwright and novelist, and is Emeritus Professor of Modern English at NUI, Galway.

SUSAN LANIGAN graduated from the M.A. in Writing at NUI, Galway with first class honours in 2003. Since then, she has had short stories published in a variety of good-quality magazines and publications, including *The Stinging Fly*, *Southword*, *The Sunday Tribune*, the *Irish Independent*, *Nature*, and *Ellery Queen Mystery Magazine*. She has been thrice shortlisted for the Hennessy New Irish Writing Award, and has been longlisted and shortlisted for the Fish Short Story Contest, the Bristol Prize, and the Raymond Carver Short Story Award.

IRINA RUPPO MALONE is a graduate of Hebrew University of Jerusalem, Trinity College Dublin, and the National University of Ireland, Galway. She is the author of *Ibsen and the Irish Revival* (Palgrave, 2010) and co-editor of *Ibsen and Chekhov on the Irish Stage* (Carysfort 2012, with and in memory of Ros Dixon). Irina teaches English Literature and Academic Writing at NUI, Galway.

MOLLY McCLOSKEY was born in Philadelphia and grew up in Oregon. In 1989, she moved to Ireland, and now divides her times between the United States and Dublin. She is the author of a collection of short stories, a novella, a novel, and one work of nonfiction, *Circles Around the Sun* (2011), which concerns her eldest brother's descent into schizophrenia. She works as an essayist, reviewer and writing teacher, has served as Writer Fellow at Trinity College Dublin, and has worked for the United Nations in the field of humanitarian assistance.

MIKE McCORMACK comes from the west of Ireland. He is the author of two collections of short stories, *Getting it in the Head* and *Forensic Songs*, and two novels, *Crowe's Requiem* and *Notes from a Coma*. Awarded the Rooney Prize for Literature in 1996, *Getting it in the Head* was also chosen as a *New York Times* Notable Book of the Year. In 2006, *Notes from a Coma* was shortlisted for the Irish Book of the Year Award. He was awarded a Civitella Ranieri Fellowship in 2007. He lives in Galway.

CONOR MONTAGUE graduated from NUI, Galway's M.A. Writing in 2008. He will shortly put a full-stop to a PhD dissertation concerning epistolary networks among cultural elites during the Irish revival. Conor recently co-edited (with Adrian Frazier) *George Moore: Dublin, Paris, Hollywood*, a collection of essays published by Irish Academic Press (2012). As well as fiction and travel narrative, Conor writes for stage and screen. His series of comedy plays, "Who Needs Enemies" have recently been adapted for television, and will be produced in the UK in 2013.

JOHN MONTAGUE is one of Ireland's foremost poets. He was born in New York and brought up in Tyrone. He has published a large number of volumes of poetry, most recently *Speech Lessons* (Gallery, 2011), two collections of short stories and two volumes of memoir. He has taught in universities in Ireland and the US and received numerous prizes and awards. In 1998 he became the first occupant of the Ireland Chair of Poetry.

PETE MULLINEAUX is a poet, dramatist and songwriter living in Galway. He teaches drama and creative writing, and is involved in development education in schools. He has written and devised numerous dramas for the stage and three plays for RTE radio, including *Butterfly Wings* (2010), co-written with Moya Roddy. Individual poems have been published in numerous anthologies, including *Landing Places* (Dedalus, 2010) and *Poems for Fathers* (about.com/poetry), among others. His collections are *Zen Traffic Lights* (Lapwing 2005), *A Father's Day*, (Salmon Poetry, 2008), and most recently *Session* (Salmon, 2011), from which "Making Rain" is taken.

VAL NOLAN teaches contemporary literature, digital media, and creative writing at NUI, Galway. He is a literary critic for the *Irish Examiner* and is currently completing a monograph on novelist/filmmaker Neil Jordan. Winner of the Penguin Ireland Short Story Competition and the *Daily Telegraph* Travel Writing Contest, his fiction has appeared in the *Irish Times*, the *Telegraph*, *Cosmos*, the *RTÉ Guide*, and the "Futures" page of the science journal *Nature*. His academic articles have appeared in *Irish Studies Review* and *Review of Contemporary Fiction*. He is a graduate of UCC, NUIG, and the Clarion Writers' Workshop at UC San Diego.

MARY O'MALLEY's latest book, *Valparaiso*, was published in 2012 by Carcanet. She is the next Humboldt Professor of Irish Studies at Villanova University. She taught for many years on the M.A. in Writing course at NUI, Galway, and is a member of Aosdána.

CHRISTIAN O'REILLY is a playwright and screenwriter based in Galway. His plays have been produced in Ireland and internationally by companies such as Druid and Rough Magic. He was a recipient of the Stewart Parker Trust New Playwright Bursary for his debut play *The Good Father* (2002). He is currently Playwright in Residence at the Town Hall Theatre, Galway. Christian is a graduate of the 2011 BBC Writers' Academy, where he was trained to write for *Doctors*, *Casualty*, *Eastenders*, and *Holby City*. His screen credits include *Inside I'm Dancing* (2004), a feature film based on his original story.

RUTH QUINLAN is from Tralee, County Kerry. She worked in IT before taking a break to complete the MA in Writing at NUI, Galway. She was shortlisted for the 2012 Cúirt New Writing fiction prize, longlisted for the 2012 Over the Edge New Writer of the Year competition, and the winner of the 2013 Hennessy First Fiction Award. She was also a Featured Reader at the February 2013 Over the Edge: Open Reading. Her work has been published by the *Irish Independent*, *Emerge Literary*

Journal, Thresholds, SIN, and *Scissors and Spackle.* She has also contributed to two group anthologies, *Abandoned Darlings* (fiction) and *Wayword Tuesdays* (poetry).

THOMAS DILLON REDSHAW is Emeritus Professor of English at the University of St. Thomas, St. Paul, Minnesota, the home of the annual O'Shaughnessy Prize for Irish Poetry. He edited the journals *Éire-Ireland* and *New Hibernia Review.* Creighton University Press published his *Well Dreams: Essays on John Montague* in 2004. During the 1990s, he spent summers out in An Cheathrú Rua getting to know Irish "as she is spoke."

MOYA RODDY lives in Galway and writes fiction, drama, poetry, as well as for television and film, and has a passion for art. Her work includes novel *The Long Way Home* (Attic Press, 1992), and the short story collection *Other People* (wordsonthestreet, 2010). Along with her short story "The Day I Gave Neil Jordan a Lift," RTÉ have broadcast two of her radio plays, "Dance Ballerina Dance" and "Butterfly Wings." She has also written for RTÉ's successful sitcom *Upwardly Mobile.* Roddy has worked for BBC, Channel 4 and Scottish Television, and has had several films optioned in America. She completed an M.A. in Writing at NUI, Galway in 2008, where she facilitates meditation weekly.

AILBHE SLEVIN completed the M.A. in Writing at NUI, Galway in 2005. She has written for the Irish language drama "Ros na Rún," and is currently working on her second novel. She lives in the Claddagh with her husband, Christian, and their two-year-old son, Cóilín.

JORDAN SMITH is the author of six collections of poetry, most recently *For Appearances, The Names of Things Are Leaving,* and *The Light in the Film,* all from the University of Tampa Press. He is the Edward E. Hale Jr., Professor of English at Union College, in upstate New York.

DEIRDRE SULLIVAN is a graduate of the M.A. in Drama and Theatre Studies at NUI, Galway. Her first novel for young adults, *Prim Improper,* was published in 2010. Her next book, *Improper Order,* was published in April 2013.

ÁINE TIERNEY holds an M.A. in Writing from the NUI, Galway. She read "My Grandmother and the Runt" at the Cúirt Over The Edge Showcase for Emerging Writers in 2010. She credits the non-fiction seminar convened by Adrian Frazier during her M.A. with helping her find her writing voice. Her comic novel, *Panacea,* was highly commended in the inaugural Irish Writers' Centre Novel Fair Competition. She is currently seeking representation for both *Panacea* and her recently completed children's book *Eat My Bad,* while working on her second adult novel, *Love Across Party Lines.*

EAMONN WALL, a native of Co. Wexford, has lived in the United States since 1982. His recent publications include *Writing the Irish West: Ecologies and Traditions* (University of Notre Dame Press, 2011) and *Sailing Lake Mareotis* (Salmon Poetry, 2011). He teaches Irish and British writing at the University of Missouri-St. Louis and spends most of his summers in Galway.

CHRISTIAN WALLACE was raised in West Texas. He completed the M.A. in Writing at the NUI, Galway in 2012. While pursuing his degree, Wallace hosted an alternative-country show on Flirt FM, and could often be found in The Crane Bar listening to tunes or playing his own songs. Music continues to be a driving force behind his work. Wallace has since returned to Texas to work, write, and take care of his dog, Loretta.

DAVID WHEATLEY is the author of four collections of poetry with Gallery Press, *Thirst* (1997), *Misery Hill* (2000), *Mocker* (2006) and *A Nest on the Waves* (2010). He has edited the work of James Clarence Mangan for Gallery Press and Samuel Beckett's *Selected Poems 1930-1989* for Faber and Faber. He edited the poetry journal *Metre* for many years with Justin Quinn.

VINCENT WOODS is a former writer in residence at NUI, Galway where he also taught drama and creative writing. His plays include *At the Black Pig's Dyke* and *A Cry from Heaven*. His poetry collections are *The Colour of Language* and *Lives and Miracles*. He presents "Arts Tonight" on RTÉ Radio 1, and is a member of Aosdána.